PRAISE FOR 25 FOR LATTER-DAY FAMILIES

"A handy reference for LDS families looking for cinematic guidance."
—Barbara Kundanis, *Library Journal*

"An essential resource for families. Sure to inspire meaningful conversations about meaningful movies."
—Kieth Merrill, Academy Award-winning director of *The Testaments*, *Legacy*, and *Mr. Krueger's Christmas*

"A marvelous tool for finding clean entertainment."
—Rebecca Baron, Mommy Bear Media

"A fantastic read, thoughtful and poignant. It will sit nicely next to my copy of Michael Medved's *Hollywood vs. America*."
—Ryan Little, director of *Saints and Soldiers*, *Forever Strong*, and *Outlaw Trail*

"Offers terrific insights about Church doctrine and media standards."
—Grady Kerr, Mormon Media Reviews

"Perfect for families. A great guide to the movies with LDS values in mind."
—Christian Vuissa, director of *Silent Night*, *The Letter Writer*, and *One Good Man*

250 GREAT MOVIES for LATTER-DAY FAMILIES

Jonathan Decker

Foreword by T.C. Christensen, director of *Ephraim's Rescue* and *17 Miracles*

CFI
An Imprint of Cedar Fort, Inc.
Springville, Utah

ISBN 13: 978-1-4621-1218-0

Published by CFI, an imprint of Cedar Fort, Inc., 2373 W. 700 S., Springville, UT 84663
Distributed by Cedar Fort, Inc., www.cedarfort.com

LIBRARY OF CONGRESS CATALOGING-IN-PUBLICATION DATA

Decker, Jonathan, 1981- author.
  250 great movies for latter-day families / Jonathan Decker.
     pages cm
  Summary: Film reviews for members of The Church of Jesus Christ of Latter-day Saints.
  ISBN 978-1-4621-1218-0
  1. Motion pictures--Reviews. I. Title. II. Title: Two hundred fifty great movies for latter-day families.

  PN1995.D374 2013
  791.43'750882893--dc23

                    2013021995

Cover design by Shawnda Craig
Cover design © 2013 Lyle Mortimer
Edited and typeset by Emily S. Chambers and Valene Wood

Printed in the United States of America

10 9 8 7 6 5 4 3 2 1

This book is dedicated to my darling wife, who supports me in everything that I do (and helps me to do it better); to my parents, who nurtured my faith in Jesus Christ; and to the artists whose work fires my imagination and enriches my life.

CONTENTS

Foreword

I love movies. I love watching them, making them, and sitting next to my daughter Tess on the couch while she holds the DVD jacket and spends more time looking at the jacket than at the movie. I still get teased for ruining all of my folks' home movies by threading the projector incorrectly (that's a nice way of saying I had no idea what I was doing but thought I did—just like now!), eventually making them unwatchable. . . all by the ripe old age of six. But my good parents never got mad at me or discouraged me from continuing with the shredding of their home movies.

I have a passion for good stories and for films in which families, especially LDS families, would find enjoyment, positive messages, and good examples. Jonathan Decker has created a great work that goes hand-in-hand with the efforts of the filmmakers who have created these types of movies.

Movies have a power to present a message on a subconscious level as well as being right in your face. Subliminal messages in films have resulted in countless good deeds, as well as those more horrific, in our society. With this book and his recommendations, Jonathan helps families to watch with awareness and realize the underlying themes and subtexts the filmmakers have placed in their projects. Thoughtfully enjoying a film with your family, then discussing its meaning and the lessons learned from characters and situations, is far more rewarding than just turning the lights back on and moving on with the rest of your day.

Over the past ten years, I have been amazed at how many people I have spoken with that have told me that Sunday is a movie day in their family—not just any old movie, but LDS films, or at the very least, films with LDS values. This book is a guide for such families. Now you can hold a guide to entertaining, yet moral, films right in your greasy little hands. What a fun and worthwhile journey this will be.

—T. C. Christensen

Introduction

LDS MEDIA STANDARDS

*"If there is anything virtuous, lovely, or of good report or
praiseworthy, we seek after these things."*
Thirteenth Article of Faith

The Power of Media

Of the many blessings stemming from living prophets and apostles
in modern times, few compare in importance to their voicing
the mind of the Lord on matters specific to the latter days. President
John Taylor taught that "Adam's revelation did not instruct Noah to
build his ark; nor did Noah's revelation tell Lot to forsake Sodom; nor
did either of these speak of the departure of the children of Israel from
Egypt. These all had revelations for themselves. . . . And so must we, or
we shall make shipwreck" (*Teachings of the Presidents of the Church—
John Taylor*, 158).

One issue of particular importance to God and His modern
prophets is the power and influence of books, movies, television, theatre, music, and the Internet. President Gordon B. Hinckley described
some of today's media in the following terms: "The flood of pornographic filth, [and] the inordinate emphasis on sex and violence are
not peculiar to North America. The situation is as bad in Europe and
in many other areas. The whole dismal picture indicates a weakening
rot seeping into the very fiber of society" ("In Opposition to Evil,"
Ensign, Sept. 2004). Elder H. Burke Peterson warned that "evil acts

are preceded by unrighteous thoughts, and unrighteous thoughts are born of vulgar stories, jokes, pictures, conversations, and a myriad of [*sic*] other evils and foolish products" ("Clean Thoughts, Pure Lives," *Ensign*, Sept. 1984).

While these statements, and others like them, are well known among the Latter-day Saints, we sometimes overlook prophetic teachings encouraging us to use media as a force for good in our lives and families. Consider the words of Elder M. Russell Ballard:

> One can still find movies and TV comedies and dramas that entertain and uplift and accurately depict the consequences of right and wrong. . . . Thus our biggest challenge is to choose wisely what we listen to and what we watch. . . . We need to take time to watch appropriate media with our children and discuss with them how to make choices that will uplift and build rather than degrade and destroy. ("Let Our Voices Be Heard," *Ensign*, Nov. 2003)

Though he warned against on-screen evil, President Hinckley was also deeply aware of media's power to inspire righteousness, having pioneered the Church's use of it during his life. He encouraged members to support good media, saying,

> While they [your children] are very young, read to them the great stories which have become immortal because of the virtues they teach. . . . When there is a good movie in town, consider going to the theater as a family. Your very patronage will give encouragement to those who wish to produce this type of entertainment. And use that most remarkable of all tools of communication, television, to enrich their lives. There is so much that is good, but it requires selectivity. . . . Let there be music in the home. If you have teenagers who have their own recordings, you will be prone to describe the sound as something other than music. Let them hear something better occasionally. Expose them to it. It will speak for itself. More appreciation will come than you may think. It may not be spoken, but it will be felt, and its influence will become increasingly manifest as the years pass. ("In Opposition to Evil," *Ensign*, Sept. 2004)

Uplift. Build. Enrich. These are the words used by prophets and apostles to describe the purpose of good media, suggesting that what makes something "good" is not simply whether or not it is "clean," but also whether it brings us closer to Christ. In seeking out media, we

Latter-day Saints often look for what is *absent* (sex, nudity, profanity, violence, and so on) and make our decisions that way. While this is important, we may not look enough at what is *present* in the media we choose. In other words, something can be inoffensive without uplifting the soul. This is the equivalent of cotton candy; it's not terribly bad for you, but it's not very good either. While cotton candy is fine as an occasional snack, something more substantial is needed to nourish the body. Similarly, while some acceptable media serves as a fine diversion, truly "good" media is media of substance, which, to paraphrase Elder Ballard, uplifts, entertains, and accurately depicts the consequences of moral choices.

President Brigham Young taught this same principle, applying it to the media of his day:

> Upon the stage of a theater can be represented in character, evil and its consequences, good and its happy results and rewards; the weakness and follies of man, the magnanimity of virtue and the greatness of truth. The stage can be made to aid the pulpit in impressing upon the minds of a community an enlightened sense of a virtuous life, also a proper horror of the enormity of sin and a just dread of its consequences. The path of sin with its thorns and pitfalls, its gins and snares can be revealed, and how to shun it. (*Discourses of Brigham Young*, 243)

Finding the Good

Clearly, there is much in art and entertainment that can inspire righteous choices and draw us nearer to God. But how do we find it? One of the great struggles of modern Latter-day Saints is finding media that conforms to our values. This is reflected in President Thomas S. Monson's sentiments: "I recall a time—and some of you here tonight will also—when the standards of most people were very similar to our standards. No longer is this true" ("Dare to Stand Alone," *Ensign*, Nov. 2011). This is clearly seen in the films of yesteryear, when *Ben-Hur*, *The Ten Commandments*, and *Chariots of Fire* earned profit and prestige, and even films that weren't overtly religious still agreed, for the most part, on what was right and wrong. Now, however, raunchy R-rated comedies draw enormous crowds, many PG-13 movies contain harsh language (along with remorseless violence and envelope-pushing sexuality), and even children's movies try to slip in edgy humor that only adults will get. What's more, men and women of faith, far from being the heroes, are now frequently portrayed as idiots, hypocrites, and fanatics.

Many Latter-day Saints are understandably disenchanted with popular entertainment in general and Hollywood in particular. To paraphrase Joseph Smith, I believe that we are sometimes kept from wholesome media because we know not where to find it (Doctrine and Covenants 123:12). This book is meant to help Mormon audiences find those films that are both clean and inspiring. In doing so, I have selected only cinema that I believe aligns with the standards of the Lord, as outlined in *For the Strength of Youth*. It is my sincere hope that this book will help Church members to find those films that will draw their souls closer to Christ. The films in this book either testify of Him directly or champion the causes and principles that He would champion. As Mormon taught, "Every thing which inviteth and enticeth to do good . . . is inspired of God" (Moroni 7:13).

That said, I cannot guarantee that you will agree with all of my opinions regarding the films listed in these pages. In the following chapter, I will explain how I came to select the movies listed here and how this book can help you to make your own informed decisions.

WHAT MAKES A GOOD MOVIE?

*"Choose wisely when using media because whatever you read,
listen to, or look at has an effect on you.
Select only media that uplifts you."*
For the Strength of Youth: Entertainment and Media

Three Components of Good Media: Artistic Merit, Wholesome Content & Gospel Parallels

In 2010 I had the idea to start my own website, *mormonmovieguy.com*, to provide Hollywood film reviews from a Latter-day Saint perspective. Several months in I developed what has become my signature review format, breaking each movie down into the three areas I believed my readers would care about: artistic merit, the presence of potentially offensive content, and how the film compared to the teachings of the gospel. Hoping to use the site to encourage study and discussion, I included scriptures and General Authority quotes with my reviews, which expanded on each film's major themes. I have continued this practice in this volume.

Some questions arise from all of this, of course. Why use this book when you can visit the website? Do you really need artistic reviews if all you want is to find something wholesome? Why give content overviews if this book supposedly only features "clean" movies? Isn't it a bit much to apply the scriptures and words of the brethren to every movie we see?

With regards to the first question, my website mostly only contains reviews since late 2010; therefore, I recommend using *mormonmovieguy.com* to find recommendations for films currently in theaters or recently made available for home entertainment. My site has reviews of everything from squeaky-clean films to PG-13 movies that I regretted seeing (I don't review R's). This book, on the other hand, reaches decades back, from the early days of cinema up to the present time. It also *only* contains films that I regard to be pure, lovely, and virtuous (see Philippians 4:8).

As for the other questions, please allow me to provide answers below.

Why Artistry Matters

A frequent complaint I hear among fellow members of the Church is that "good" movies are often not *good* movies. This is to say that cinema that promotes faith, marriage, family, honesty, and other virtues is often poorly acted, painfully written, and shoddily directed. The word *cheesy* is often mentioned. Those who crave compelling stories, well-rounded characters, creative filmmaking, and believable acting often look to movies whose values do not correspond with their own.

When it comes to cinema, we ought to seek out and support those efforts that excel both in moral *and* artistic quality. These are the films that have power to bring souls to the Savior, and here's why: their intentions combine with emotional authenticity, which allows audiences to see the real-world applications of eternal truths. Solid writing, directing, and acting enables audiences to relate to the person on screen and the effect of true principles on such a character resonate far more with viewers than do the effects of the same principles on a one-dimensional caricature who doesn't talk, think, feel, or act like a real person.

Furthermore, beautiful cinematography, inspiring music, and thoughtful editing all combine to create an experience that stirs the soul. This is not audience manipulation, but rather the efforts of artists whose respect for the material inspires them to give their very best. President Spencer W. Kimball echoed this sentiment:

> We must recognize that excellence and quality are a reflection of how we feel about ourselves and about life and about God. If we don't care much about these basic things, then such not caring carries over into the work we do, and our work becomes shabby and shoddy. Real

craftsmanship, regardless of the skill involved, reflects real caring, and real caring reflects our attitude about ourselves, about our fellowmen, and about life. ("The Gospel Vision of the Arts," *Ensign*, Sept. 1977)

Film can offer such craftsmanship and care. It is not mere entertainment—it is an art form, and not a lesser one. All other kinds of art are united together in movies. Cinematography uses light, color, and vivid imagery in many of the same ways as photography and painting. Production design invokes the shapes and forms of architecture and sculpture. The soul-stirring sounds of a symphony performing a film score can rival renowned classical music. Screenwriting, at its finest, draws from the power of poetry, profoundly uses symbolism, and develops character and story like a good book would. Wardrobe design combines fashion with character development. Riveting dramatic performances and riotous comedic turns rival any acting found on stage. Excellent editing provides a lesson in using structure and timing to create a desired emotional effect. Musicals can give us vocal displays of the highest order, while dancing, stunt work, and visual effects offer an artistry all their own.

Learning to pay attention to these things engages the mind and enriches the viewing experience. Therefore, in this book I will only include films that are well-made. This is why all of the reviews found here are of films which I grade a B- or above artistically (with the exception of *The Phantom Menace*, because the other *Star Wars* films are in here and, well, I'm a completist). There are plenty of "clean" movies out there to which I would assign a lower artistic grade; they just didn't make the cut for this book.

Why This Book Still Needs Content Overviews

Of course, a movie can be artistically rich but morally bankrupt; the Academy honors many of them every year! It is the aim of this book, then, to find those films that balance artistry with morality. They engage the mind and heart while nourishing the soul with positive messages and "clean" content. But who is to say what is "clean" when it comes to movies? That's easy: the Lord himself has spoken on this issue, through living prophets, in a pamphlet titled *For the Strength of Youth*. President Thomas S. Monson emphasized that this pamphlet, despite its title, isn't just for youth. He explained that "it features standards from the writings and teachings of Church leaders and from scripture, adherence to which will bring the blessings of our Heavenly Father and the guidance of His Son to each of us" ("Preparation Brings Blessings," *Ensign*, May 2010; emphasis added).

What *For the Strength of Youth* has to say about entertainment and media may give pause to many members of the Church, all of whom are expected to follow its standards: "Do not attend, view, or participate in anything that is vulgar, immoral, violent, or pornographic in any way. Do not participate in anything that presents immorality or violence as acceptable" ("Entertainment and Media," *For the Strength of Youth*). I admit that I have been deeply challenged by this counsel. Many of the films that I love are action-driven and therefore present violence as acceptable in some way or another. I didn't want to give these movies up, yet I was determined to do as Alma directed his son Helaman, namely to "be diligent in keeping the commandments of God as they are written" (Alma 37:20).

For a time I developed something of a complex; everything I watched had to comply, to the letter, with the Lord's law regarding media. A single punch in a movie, the presence of mild language in a book, would result in intense feelings of guilt. This came to a head when my father took me to the Utah Shakespeare Festival, where we attended a performance of the musical *Camelot*. I squirmed in my seat as Guinevere cheerfully celebrated vice in the tune "The Lusty Month of May." When Lancelot crooned the song "If Ever I Would Leave You" (about his unyielding love for Guinevere) I was disgusted that this play romanticized his adulterous feelings. I wanted to walk out and was deeply troubled that my father seemed totally fine with it all. Thankfully, several months later President Monson would shed welcome light on the subject and shift my paradigm in a major way.

Speaking at a fireside at Brigham Young University, President Monson cited the very play that had left me so unsettled. He said: "In your quest for the man or woman of your dreams, you may well heed the counsel given by King Arthur in the musical *Camelot*. Faced with a particularly vexing dilemma, King Arthur could well have been speaking to all of us when he declared, 'We must not let our passions destroy our dreams.' May you follow this most essential counsel" ("Decisions

Determine Destiny," CES Fireside, November 6, 2005). That a prophet of God could quote *Camelot* as a positive influence shook my assumptions to the core and led to some prayerful rethinking on my part. I realized that even though some of the songs seemingly condoned immorality, ultimately the romanticized vice was revealed to be the characters' ignorant justifications. The tragic consequences of putting desire before virtue came crashing down on them. It wasn't an "evil" play after all. It was a *morality* play. *This is powerful stuff!* I thought. Further reflection led me to recall something I had once heard from a BYU film professor: "The portrayal of something is not the same thing as condoning it." I realized that, in art and entertainment, sometimes darkness must be portrayed in order to contrast it with the light. There is no good without evil, and both must be depicted for righteousness to be promoted.

Elder Jeffrey R. Holland conveyed this principle when sharing his personal opinion on the Harry Potter series. In a 2006 speech at the Fourth Annual Guardian of Light Award Dinner, Elder Holland said:

> You are well aware of the Harry Potter books and movies by J. K. Rowling. One of the reasons the books are so popular, I think, is that they show children victorious in battle against dark forces. They give readers hope that, even in total darkness, there is that spark of light. Despite the powerful evil arrayed against them, they know they can defeat the darkness. But fundamental to the message of the Harry Potter books is the idea that children don't—indeed, can't—fight their battles alone. In fact, the one gift that saves Harry over and over again is the love of his mother, who died protecting him from evil. Without any question one of those best "defenses against the dark arts"—to use a phrase from the Harry Potter books—is close family ties. Parental love, family activity, gentle teaching, and respectful conversation—sweet time together—can help keep the generations close and build bonds that will never be broken. ("Let There Be Light," May 3, 2006)

Now, I know that many Latter-day Saints have strong feelings about Harry Potter, both for and against. I'm not implying that what Elder Holland said was anything more than his opinion. What I *am* pointing out is that he saw value in a series that isn't always sunny and pleasant, nor does it follow *For the Strength of Youth* to the letter. For example, Harry Potter has violent confrontations and some uses of language. Similarly, in general conference, Elder Quentin L. Cook called the movie *Amazing Grace*, which is about the abolition of slavery in England, "an inspiring movie" ("Let There Be Light," *Ensign*, Nov. 2010), even though that film has some language.

To be clear, I am not accusing the Brethren of hypocrisy, nor does their appreciation of Harry Potter and *Amazing Grace* necessarily constitute apostolic endorsements. I do, however, put great stock in their words, as I assume you do. This raises an interesting question as to whether the counsel regarding media in *For the Strength of Youth* is hard, uncompromising law. I believe Elder Dallin H. Oaks gives us the answer:

> As a General Authority, it is my responsibility to preach general principles. When I do, I don't try to define all the exceptions. There are exceptions to some rules. . . . But don't ask me to give an opinion on your exception. I only teach the general rules. Whether an exception applies to you is your responsibility. You must work that out individually between you and the Lord. ("The Dedication of a Lifetime," CES Fireside, May 1, 2005)

Although Elder Oaks wasn't speaking specifically about media, I believe that this principle applies to the topic. His words are both liberating and sobering. If we read them closely, we see that we cannot simply excuse ourselves from following the teachings of Christ, His apostles, and His prophets. Violence, vulgarity, immorality, and pornography still drive away the Spirit and are displeasing to the Lord. That still holds. But our agency is intact, as is God's insistence that He won't "command [us] in all things" (Doctrine and Covenants 58:26). We have been given the gift of the Holy Ghost to guide us, and we will be responsible to the Lord for how well we follow the Spirit in discerning legitimate exceptions from our own justifications.

In the case of the media guidelines given in *For the Strength of Youth*, we can clearly see the application of Elder Oaks's teaching about general principles and exceptions. Pornography, for example, is clearly *never* acceptable, as its express purpose is to arouse illicit desires and rob sexuality of its sacred nature. Not all portrayals of violence, on the other hand, encourage viewers to act aggressively or dilute their ability to feel compassion. For example, the film *The Testaments of One*

Fold and One Shepherd contains a fairly bloody depiction of the Lord's scourging and crucifixion. *Joseph Smith: the Prophet of the Restoration* portrays the death of the Prophet in a barrage of bullets. The seminary videos *The Whole Armor of God, Firm in the Faith of Christ,* and *O Ye Fair Ones,* produced for adolescents and young adults in seminary and institute programs, contain stabbings with swords, soldiers shot with arrows, and rivers flowing with blood. Overzealous application of counsel regarding violent media could lead members to shun faith-promoting films produced by their own church.

Context matters in selecting media. The purpose of the violence in *The Testaments* and in the Joseph Smith film is, respectively, to increase appreciation for the Atonement of Jesus Christ and for the martyrdom of Brother Joseph. In *O Ye Fair Ones,* the bloody aftermath is meant to display the tragic consequences of the Nephites abandoning God. *The Whole Armor of God* uses a battle scene to visually illustrate the Apostle Paul's metaphor of our battle with sin. *Firm in the Faith of Christ* portrays the righteous warfare of Captain Moroni, who didn't delight in bloodshed but was willing to forcibly defend the faith, families, and freedom of the Nephites from tyranny and oppression. It's worth pointing out that none of these films is needlessly graphic nor glamorizes aggression and hate.

This leads back to the topic of why this book has content reviews of its movies. While every movie reviewed here has been personally selected as virtuous and in keeping with the Lord's standards, that judgment is merely my opinion. I've purposely avoided anything pornographic, excessively crass and profane, or gratuitously violent, but some of the films herein may have scenes that are mildly vulgar or have non-graphic, purposeful violence such as self-defense, defending the innocent, or learning the tragic consequences of vengeance.

This book is not meant to be seen as a guaranteed list of movies that all members will agree upon, though I've tried to seek the guidance of the Holy Ghost in choosing inspiring films that many Latter-day Saints would feel comfortable watching. That said, I cannot predict what might offend you personally. You may take exception to the warfare and mild language of the PG-13 *Saints and Soldiers.* Perhaps you'll find the presence of sport bikinis in the PG-rated Christian film *Soul Surfer* unacceptable. You might not want your children subjected to

Mufasa's death in *The Lion King* or to the comic use of the word *butt* in *Finding Nemo*, regardless of their G-ratings. On the other hand, you might not be fazed by any of those things. I don't know because I'm not you. What I've tried to do with the content overviews is to give you accurate information regarding potentially offensive content, allowing you to make your own decisions.

I hasten to add that just because a film doesn't appear here doesn't necessarily mean that it's "bad" or not worthwhile. For example, I personally was inspired by 2008's *The Dark Knight*. I appreciated that, when challenged by a madman, the hero and others stood their ground. Displaying selflessness and courage, their morality withstood tragedy and fear. However, I know many people thought that the film, because of its menacing villain and dark tone, was sadistic and unwatchable. Since I have no intention of debating the point or causing controversy, I'll not include such a divisive film here. The first *Pirates of the Caribbean* movie is another example. To me the film is harmless escapist fun, while to others the fact that a pirate is the charming and funny antihero is distasteful and dangerous. Again, in order to focus solely on movies that I believe most Latter-day Saints can agree upon, it's not included here.

Furthermore, there are hundreds, perhaps thousands, of wholesome films spanning decades and continents that I've not yet seen and thus haven't included. Feel free to seek them out. This book is not meant to be the final word on good movies. It is only meant to assist you in making quality film choices. You, no doubt, can think of many other movies worth including here. So can I, but I didn't have the space or the time to rewatch and review them all. If this volume is successful, however, there may be a second volume with 250 *more* excellent choices, so if you enjoy the book, please suggest to your friends that they buy a copy as well!

Using the Scripture Verses, Hymns, and General Authority Quotes

More important than artistry and more important than content is whether the films we watch draw us nearer to the Lord. This is not to suggest that we should watch only somber, reverent films. Silly, funny entertainment can still be rich with moral instruction (that's one reason why we love *VeggieTales* in my home). If we choose good media, we can be instructed in truth whether the filmmakers share our faith or not.

Elder Boyd K. Packer explains why this is. He taught that "every man, woman, and child of every nation, creed, or color—everyone, no matter where they live or what they believe or what they do—has within them the imperishable Light of Christ. . . . [It] can enlighten the inventor, the scientist, the painter, the sculptor, the composer, the performer, the architect, the author to produce great, even inspired things for the blessing and good of all mankind" ("The Light of Christ," *Liahona*, Apr. 2005). This certainly also applies to filmmakers, as they too are children of God and thus inheritors of this divine gift. To the extent that they follow the light within themselves, their work can motivate, inspire, and lead to truth.

To know how we can best harness the power of movie-watching to provide spiritual edification, we need look no further than the scriptures. We read in the Bible: "Trust in the Lord with all thy heart. . . . In all thy ways acknowledge him, and he shall direct thy paths" (Proverbs 3:5–6). Alma advised Helaman to "let all thy doings be unto the Lord, and whithersoever thou goest let it be in the Lord; yea, let all thy thoughts be directed unto the Lord" (Alma 37:36). Certainly even when watching film can we direct our thoughts toward the Lord. Through the truths we glean from movies, we can learn to trust more in Him. In my experience, this doesn't take away from one's enjoyment of cinema; it enriches it.

To that end, I refer to scripture verses and quotes by General Authorities of the Church with each review. These expound upon the films' major themes (as I see them) and provide a springboard for discussion and study. In this way, movie-watching ceases to be a passive activity, becoming instead an active and engaging pursuit. Of course, you may simply want to turn your brain off and escape for a couple of hours, and that's fine too. The verses and quotes are still there if you decide to use them. To be clear, these are only meant to stimulate conversation and thought and are not in any way a claim that my thoughts are the final word on a film's meaning or moral. You may see themes that I overlooked or meanings that are personal to you because of your life experiences. All

I'm trying to do is get you thinking, examining, and talking.

Some of the most profound gospel conversations I've ever had have come after watching a film and drawing eternal truths out of it. I sincerely hope that this book helps you to do the same. I pray that the movies you choose and the conversations that you have, in some small part because of this book, strengthen your faith in our Savior Jesus Christ and solidify your resolve to keep His commandments. Though I'm an imperfect man, I seek to align my intentions with those of Nephi, who said, "The fulness of mine intent is that I may persuade men to come unto the God of Abraham, and the God of Isaac, and the God of Jacob, and be saved" (1 Nephi 6:4). I realize that this may seem overly ambitious for a book of movie reviews, but I know that "by small and simple things are great things brought to pass" (Alma 37:6).

HOW TO USE THIS BOOK

As you read in the previous chapter, artistic merit, agreeable content, and the presence of eternal truths are the criteria I've used to select the films reviewed in this book. As I've noted, each review is broken down and assessed in those three areas. The artistic reviews speak for themselves. The "messages to discuss" sections provide my thoughts on the gospel truths conveyed by each movie with references to scriptures and General Authority quotes to jump-start your own gospel discussions.

With regards to the content overviews, I'd like to clarify the terms I use. *Vulgarity* refers to uses of words and phrases such as "crap," "p*ssed off" and "butt." *Innuendo* refers to any comments of a sexual nature. Most films in this book have neither, but there are rare exceptions where some have the mildest forms. For example, in the G-rated film *Babe*, a duck destined for the butcher's block laments that "humans don't eat roosters—why? They make eggs with the hens and wake everyone up in the morning. I tried it with the hens: it didn't work." A handful of films here have one or two *moderate* innuendos, and I've tried to make sure to point them out. In the otherwise wholesome and PG-rated *Father of the Bride,* for example, Steve Martin is worried about his engaged daughter and blurts out a suggestion that she practice safe sex, much to her embarrassment. In such rare cases, where I believe that the overall value of the film outweighs such a moment, I still include warnings so you can make your own educated choice.

In terms of profanity, I've mostly included only films that have no foul language at all. With the rare exceptions that do, I classify profanity using the following system: *Mild profanity* is use of the words "hell, damn, a**, and "god" (little "g" as I reserve the capital "G" for the reverent version) used in inappropriate ways. *Moderate profanity* is almost anything else, other than the f-word, which I classify as *harsh* profanity. I've included no films with harsh profanity here, though I think some films with harsh profanity (like *Of Gods and Men* and *World Trade Center*) are still worthwhile. The film *The Blind Side*, for example, contains strong positive depictions of marriage, family, and Christianity, but has two or three moderate profanities. In cases that concern individuals and families, they may choose to use content filters, such as a *ClearPlay* DVD player or a *TV Guardian*, or to skip these films entirely. Again, the content overview is there to help you make your decision.

With regards to sexuality, I've made sure that no film in the book contains any "love scenes" or sexual nudity. In rare cases there is wardrobe that some might consider immodest while others would find it contextually appropriate. One such case is the Christian drama *End of the Spear*, which features tribal natives in loincloths with the males practically exposing their backsides. It is an historically accurate, Christ-centered film that I would be totally comfortable watching with the Savior in the room. Some films address sexuality in an appropriately mature fashion, arguably making them suitable for teens and up. For example, in the 1998 film *Les Miserables,* the ailing prostitute Fantine (Uma Thurman) offers herself to kindly Jean Valjean (Liam Neeson) as a token of gratitude for nursing her back to health. He displays true virtue when he refuses her offer and instead expresses pure Christian love and concern for her well-being. He comforts her in her affliction, telling her that God is a loving Father who doesn't see her as a whore but as His beautiful child. This, to me, is an appropriate inclusion of sexual themes.

As for violence, I've gone out of my way to include nothing that is graphic or gratuitous, although some films may contain violence (or its aftermath) that I believe is contextually appropriate. This is to say that it is portrayed in the context of self-defense, protecting the innocent, or conveying the tragic consequences of improper force. *Life is Beautiful* has a haunting scene in which the protagonist finds stacks of Jewish bodies in a Nazi concentration camp (obscured somewhat by fog). *The Lord of the Rings* has warriors defending their homes and families. *Star Wars: Episode III—Revenge of the Sith* portrays Anakin Skywalker going on a killing spree, but this is portrayed as heartbreaking and soul-destroying, not glamorous or "cool." The content overviews will help you decide if, and with whom, you choose to watch these movies. Similarly, a few films have characters who smoke or drink, usually portrayed as harmful, and I'm sure to let you know about it.

The book's structure is simple: there are 250 films listed in alphabetical order. In the back of the book, you'll find several indexes to help you find what you're looking for. If you want to search for films by genre, rating, or gospel topic (such as "repentance"), you can use these accompanying indexes for each of those categories. Now, without any further ado, let's dive into those reviews!

The Movie Reviews

(In alphabetical order by name of movie)

12 DOGS OF CHRISTMAS: GREAT PUPPY RESCUE (PG, 2012)

It's tough to pull off a good dog movie. Fortunately, director Kieth Merrill (*The Testaments, Legacy, Mr. Krueger's Christmas*) brings his artistic sensibilities to the table with *12 Dogs of Christmas: Great Puppy Rescue*, which works as both a standalone film and as a sequel to his original *12 Dogs of Christmas* (2005). Emma returns to save the dogs of Doverville from losing their home (and consequently being either put to sleep or turned into racing animals), putting on a fundraiser performance to save the puppy orphanage. It's a simple, straightforward family film, but what it does, it does very well, giving further evidence to Roger Ebert's famous assertion that "it's not the story you tell, but how you tell it." With a charming lead performance by Dani Chuchran (who gives her character spunk, warmth, and wit) and solid supporting work by Heather Beers (*Charly, Baptists at our Barbeque*), and D. B. Sweeney (*The Cutting Edge*), as well as a host of young actors and cuddly canines, the characters are better-realized than in other films in the genre. Sean Patrick Flannery (*The Young Indiana Jones Chronicles*) comes across as more of a one-dimensional villain, but that's par for the course. The attention to detail in recreating the look of the 1930s in clothing, props, and sets is impressive, and the song-and-dance numbers provide some real razzle-dazzle. *12 Dogs of Christmas: Great Puppy Rescue* is a well-crafted, well-acted, warm-hearted holiday movie that goes down as easily as a mug of hot chocolate. Families will enjoy it immensely.

GRADE: B

CONTENT OVERVIEW: It has no violence, sexuality, or language. There's an accident scene and some moments of puppies in peril, but the film is designed to be appropriate for all ages.

MESSAGES TO DISCUSS: We all have different gifts and talents, and if we unite them by working together, we can accomplish great things (1 Corinthians 12:4–27). Dogs can be wonderful friends and sources of comfort (Luke 16:21).

17 MIRACLES (PG, 2011)

T. C. Christensen's moving account of the Willie-Martin handcart companies may be the best film yet from Mormon cinema. It displays with historical accuracy and emotional honesty the great challenges of imperfect people whose trials refined their characters and whose faith wrought divine intervention. Though the movie, due to its structure, can't help but feel episodic, it is gripping history nonetheless. The music, cinematography, costume design, and attention to detail are all top notch.

GRADE: A

CONTENT OVERVIEW: There are implications of cannibalism as the remains of the Donner Party are found (nothing graphic is shown). There is plenty of suffering, starvation, frozen corpses, and other thematic elements inherent to the handcart story. It is intense, but historically accurate, and contains absolutely nothing offensive. Appropriate for older children and up.

MESSAGES TO DISCUSS: There are far too many to list here, but two that spring to mind: the mercies of the Lord are over all those who have faith in Him (1 Nephi 1:20) and after much tribulation come blessings (Doctrine and Covenants 58:2–4).

101 DALMATIANS (G, 1961)

This ever-charming Disney classic is about a musician, his wife, and their pet dalmatians facing off against the villainous fashionista Cruella De Vil and her insidious plot to make coats out of dog fur. Highlighted by a jazz music score, adorable characters, and plenty of daring escapes, this is one all generations can enjoy.

GRADE: A-

CONTENT OVERVIEW: The musician smokes a pipe, and Cruella smokes a cigarette from a long, thin cigarette holder. Henchmen are kicked in the rear by a horse, and one of their behinds catches on fire when he falls into a fireplace. When a female dog delivers a large litter, the musician proudly calls the male dog an "old rascal."

MESSAGES TO DISCUSS: There is strength in numbers, unity, and teamwork (Ecclesiastes 4: 9–12).

20,000 LEAGUES UNDER THE SEA (G, 1954)

This terrific live-action Disney adaptation of the classic Jules Verne novel finds two nineteenth-century sailors and a professor as shipwrecked guests/prisoners of Nemo, captain of an incredible submarine, who patrols the oceans in an attempt to both escape the world and avenge its wrongs. All these years later, the adventure still pops, as do the visual effects, while the tragic morality tale hasn't lost any of its potency.

GRADE: A-

CONTENT OVERVIEW: There is no language or sexuality, though Kirk Douglas often goes shirtless and says once that he wants to meet some "native girls hungry for affection." There are some fistfights, some shootings with mild blood, and a fairly intense confrontation with a giant squid on the ocean's surface. A few characters smoke and drink.

MESSAGES TO DISCUSS: The Lord gives us knowledge according to our ability to apply it morally (2 Nephi 28:29–30); the oceans and the wonders therein are creations of God (Genesis 1:10, 21–22).

5000 DAYS PROJECT, THE: TWO BROTHERS (NR, 2012)

With *Two Brothers*, documentary filmmaker Rick Stevenson (a Protestant) launches the decade-in-the-making *5000 Days Project*, an interfaith effort to capture the struggles, hopes, fears, and achievements of two hundred children in six countries over the years. The film follows Sam and Luke Nelson, Seattle siblings and Latter-day Saints whose real-life story includes such relatable trials as loneliness, self-doubt, and family tension, as well as cinema-ready adversities such as fighting depression, reaching for the dream of playing college football, and coping with catastrophic natural disaster. Through it all, the boys' personalities, faith in Jesus Christ, and compassion for others make for an imminently watchable documentary.

GRADE: A

CONTENT OVERVIEW: *Two Brothers* is unrated, but contains nothing offensive and could carry a G rating.

MESSAGES TO DISCUSS: The Lord gives us weaknesses to make us humble, and if we humble ourselves and have faith in Him, weaknesses will turn to strengths (Ether 12:27). Developing a Christlike love means developing compassion that will cause us to feel heartache for the pains of others (John 11:35; 2 Nephi 33:3). This love, and pain, ultimately brings the greatest joys (3 Nephi 17:20). Servants of Christ love and serve others (Mark 9:35, John 13:34–35). Standing for the Savior sometimes means standing alone (Helaman 10:1). Family difficulties can be overcome (1 John 2:10, Mosiah 4:14–15).

ABSENT-MINDED PROFESSOR, THE (NR, 1961)

This funny and, pardon the pun, *inventive* comedy from Disney finds a socially inept scientist using his bouncy creation (Flubber) to save the university and win back his estranged fiancé. The performances have a "gee-whiz" innocence that is undeniably likable, while the clever editing, stunt work, and visual effects create iconic scenes (a flying car, a high-bounding basketball team) that retain their impressiveness today.

GRADE: A-

CONTENT OVERVIEW: With Flubber on his shoes, the professor bounces over two thugs, who keep crashing headfirst into things.

MESSAGES TO DISCUSS: Things of great worth should be used for a righteous cause and protected from those who'd use them selfishly or harmfully (Joseph Smith—History 1:60).

ADVENTURES OF ICHABOD AND MR. TOAD (G, 1949)

Basil Rathbone and Bing Crosby narrate these dual animated tales. The first, "The Wind in the Willows," tells the tale of a fad-obsessed frog whose greed for a new car lands him in hot water. The second, "The Legend of Sleepy Hollow," is a Halloween favorite: New England school professor Ichabod Crane competes with a local alpha male for a woman's affections, finding himself face-to-face with the dreaded Headless Horseman in the spooky woods. It's a lot of fun.

GRADE: B+

CONTENT OVERVIEW: A song about the Headless Horseman, as well as the actual encounter with him in the woods, may be frightening to small children.

MESSAGES TO DISCUSS: "Once in debt, interest is your companion every minute of the day and night; you cannot shun it or slip away from it; you cannot dismiss it; it yields neither to entreaties, demands, or orders; and whenever you get in its way or cross its course or fail to meet its demands, it crushes you" (President J. Reuben Clark, in

Conference Report, Apr. 1938, 103). We do not need to be afraid of anything because God is with us (Isaiah 41:13).

ADVENTURES OF ROBIN HOOD, THE (PG, 1938)

Often considered to be the definitive Robin Hood film, this features the dashing Errol Flynn in the title role. With charisma to spare, he woos Lady Marion, robs the rich while giving to the poor, and thwarts Prince John in this faithful adaptation of the classic legend. Boasting terrific stunts, exciting sword fights, old-Hollywood romance, dazzling sets, and bold interpretations of the characters, this is one for film buffs and lovers of adventure.

GRADE: B+

CONTENT OVERVIEW: A few kissing scenes. Some characters drink wine. Numerous characters die from arrows to the chest or in sword fights (bloodless).

MESSAGES TO DISCUSS: "That which is wrong under one circumstance may be, and often is, right under another" (Joseph Smith, in *The Personal Writings of Joseph Smith*, Dean C. Jessee [editor], p. 507–9). When wicked persons try to usurp power and destroy liberty, we are justified in opposing them (Alma 46:10–21). The Lord expects us to help the poor (Luke 14:13–14).

ADVENTURES OF TINTIN, THE (PG, 2011)

Director Steven Spielberg and producer Peter Jackson team up to give us a terrific family adventure: an adaptation of a popular European comic book series about a young reporter and the mysteries he solves. It's part *Indiana Jones*, part *Hardy Boys*, and part *Pirates of the Caribbean*. Though the story lacks much emotional draw, it's got plenty of humor, phenomenal animation, and the best action scenes of its kind since *The Incredibles*.

GRADE: B+

CONTENT OVERVIEW: A supporting character's alcoholism is a consistent plot point, so parents may want to address the topic of drinking with their children. Hard drinking is portrayed as a negative character trait. There are a couple of mild profanities. A character is shot off screen and bleeds slightly. There's plenty of punching, kicking, shootouts, and swordplay, though only in a pirate-themed flashback does anybody die.

MESSAGES TO DISCUSS: "Perseverance is a positive, active characteristic. It is not idly, passively waiting and hoping for some good thing to happen. It gives us hope by helping us realize that the righteous suffer no failure except in giving up and no longer trying" (Wirthlin, Joseph B. "Never Give Up," *Ensign,* Nov. 1987).

ALADDIN (G, 1992)

This quintessential Disney animated classic is about the Arabian street urchin, the princess he loves, and the genie of the magic lamp who grants him three wishes. Though many remember the seminal vocal work of Robin Williams as the genie, there's much more to enjoy here, not least of which is the Oscar-winning music by Alan Menkin and Tim Rice. Entertaining from start to finish.

GRADE: A

CONTENT OVERVIEW: The heroine and several other females wear clothing that reveals midriffs and mild cleavage; some of the women shake their hips sensually. A merchant threatens to cut a woman's hand off. After turning into a giant snake, the villain is stabbed by the hero.

MESSAGES TO DISCUSS: All secrets come out sooner or later (2 Nephi 30:17; Luke 8:17). We need to keep our promises, as the Lord does with us (1 Kings 8:56).

ALICE IN WONDERLAND (G, 1951)

This always-amusing Disney adaptation of Lewis Carroll's *Alice's Adventures in Wonderland* finds British girl Alice, bored with reality and engaging in a series of adventures in an imaginative wonderland. It's random and delightfully silly, with unforgettable characters.

GRADE: B+

CONTENT OVERVIEW: An evil queen threatens the heroine with beheading. A scene that is both sad and funny finds a walrus luring baby oysters away from their mother and eating them. The heroine drinks potions that affect her body size.

MESSAGES TO DISCUSS: While imagination can be a wonderful thing, we must also make time to live in, and enjoy, reality (1 Corinthians 13:11). Honor and obey your parents; they're trying to protect you (Exodus 20:12; 1 Nephi 8:37). Beware those who speak flattering words (Proverbs 26:28; Mosiah 26:6).

AMAZING GRACE (PG, 2006)

Handsomely shot and impeccably acted, *Amazing Grace* portrays the real-life struggles of English statesman William Wilberforce, who led the charge to abolish slavery in eighteenth-century Great Britain, as well as the stories of those who inspired him (including reformed slave-ship captain and man of God John Newton, who penned the titular hymn). Despite being a bit slowly paced at times, this is a marvelous film that may give you both tears and chills.

GRADE: B+

CONTENT OVERVIEW: There is some mild language. Crippled persons without fingers or legs are shown. A man shows his scars from being branded a slave and describes the torturous conditions suffered by slaves, including rape, being buried alive, illness, and dying at sea.

MESSAGES TO DISCUSS: Slavery is against the will of God (Doctrine and Covenants 101:79–80; Alma 27:9). The story of William Wilberforce is related by Elder Quentin L. Cook in his October 2010 general conference talk, titled "Let There Be Light."

AMERICAN IN PARIS, AN (NR, 1951)

This classic finds Gene Kelly as a struggling painter who starts a romance with a young Frenchwoman, not knowing that she's engaged. The love story lacks spark, but the song-and-dance numbers are terrific and the production design is lavish.

GRADE: B

CONTENT OVERVIEW: There are a few sultry dance moves but, this being the 1950s, things don't get out of hand.

MESSAGES TO DISCUSS: If you love someone, you put their wants and needs before your own (Philippians 2:3–4)

AMERICAN PROPHET: THE STORY OF JOSEPH SMITH (NR, 1999)

Detail-rich and even-handed, this PBS documentary about the life of Joseph Smith contains numerous insights from scholars within and without the Church, General Authorities, and firsthand accounts from journals and letters of the era. Supplemented with lovely music and plenty of photography/artwork, this is a professionally crafted, faith-promoting work given extra heft by the gravitas of narration by Hollywood legend Gregory Peck (*Roman Holiday, Moby Dick*). I highly recommend this movie.

GRADE: A-

CONTENT OVERVIEW: This film contains no offensive material.

MESSAGES TO DISCUSS: The Prophet Joseph Smith has done more for the salvation of humanity than anyone else who has ever lived, with the exception of the Savior Jesus Christ (Doctrine and Covenants 135:3). He is both revered and derided (Joseph Smith—History 1:33).

AMISH GRACE (TV-PG, 2010)

Despite its status as a Lifetime movie and criticisms that it takes artistic liberties with actual events, *Amish Grace* emerges as a poignant and inspiring little movie. It tells the story of the 2006 massacre of Amish schoolchildren by a mentally unstable gunman, the community's subsequent forgiveness of the murderer, and their outreach to his widow. Due largely to acting and screenwriting that are far better than expected, the film transcends its made-for-TV cinematography, editing, and musical score. Ideally it will motivate viewers to learn more about the actual events.

GRADE: B

CONTENT OVERVIEW: *Amish Grace* tastefully addresses the true story of the massacre of Amish schoolchildren by a mentally unstable gunman. The shootings occur off screen, and though the characters see the bodies, the audience does not. Though it contains nothing offensive and is appropriate for families, the film is thematically intense as it deals with the emotional and spiritual aftermath of murder, so parents should be ready to discuss the story with mature children.

MESSAGES TO DISCUSS: The Lord asks us to forgive others so that our sins may be forgiven (Matthew 6:14–15). Forgiveness doesn't mean condoning wrong actions or letting someone escape consequences; it means letting go of bitterness and hate, allowing God to be the perfect judge (Doctrine and Covenants 64:9–11). We are commanded to love our enemies (Matthew 5:43–48).

ARTIST, THE (PG-13, 2011)

A modern silent film in the style of classic Hollywood, *The Artist* hearkens back to the days of Charlie Chaplin and Buster Keaton, an era when comedy and emotion were conveyed purely through physical acting, and human movement was the only special effect needed. The film follows a silent film star who becomes irrelevant with the advent of "talkies" (movies with sound) and his subsequent rescue from despair by the love and friendship of a good woman. It's a bit slow in the middle, but, overall, *The Artist* is terrifically moving, uplifting, creative, and fun, as well as romantic in a tender, pure-hearted way that is all but lost from modern cinema. Winner of an Oscar for Best Picture.

GRADE: A

CONTENT OVERVIEW: A woman gives a man "the bird," a man contemplates suicide and puts a gun into his mouth, and there is one mild profanity. There is some smoking and drinking. It arguably could have been PG. (Spoiler) A married man and a single woman feel romantic chemistry but do not act on it until years later when he's divorced.

MESSAGES TO DISCUSS: Pride and arrogance lead to failure (Proverbs 16:18). Treat others as you would like to be treated (Luke 6:31). True love is more than chemistry and attraction; it is kindness, patience, endurance, and taking care of each other (1 Corinthians 13:4–5). "Forgiveness, with love and tolerance, accomplishes miracles that can happen in no other way" (Hinckley, Gordon B. "Forgiveness," *Ensign,* Nov. 2005). Life can compel us to be humble, which leads to obtaining mercy (Alma 32:13).

ARTHUR CHRISTMAS (PG, 2011)

If given the chance, this hilarious animated film will be a new Christmas classic, combining as it does a madcap sense of humor with a warm heart. The film takes as its central premise that the Clauses are a multigenerational family, with the mantle of "Santa" inherited from father to son. It follows the misadventures of the current Santa's son, a well-meaning misfit named Arthur, as he struggles to deliver a gift to the one child on earth who was accidentally overlooked on Christmas Eve. The film benefits from fine pacing and wall-to-wall creativity as it turns the Santa Claus legend on its head. This is feel-good family entertainment; smart, sassy, and heartfelt.

GRADE: A-

CONTENT OVERVIEW: *Arthur Christmas* is rated PG, though for the life of me I can't imagine why. Even with some moments of peril, this is a G-rated film all the way. There is nothing objectionable here.

MESSAGES TO DISCUSS: Just as every child matters to the one true Santa in the film, in real life every single person matters to the one true God (Doctrine and Covenants 18:10–11, Luke 15:4–7). Families, like the Church of Jesus Christ, have need of every member, with their different strengths and talents, doing their part (1 Corinthians 12:12–26). "No other success in life can compensate for failure in the home" (President David O. McKay, quoting from J. E. McCullough, Home: The Savior of Civilization [1924], 42; Conference Report, Apr. 1935, 116).

AVENGERS, THE (PG-13, 2012)

With a witty screenplay, charismatic performances, and wall-to-wall action, Marvel Studios's *The Avengers* is a thrilling crowd pleaser. The film finds Iron Man, Thor, The Hulk, Captain America, and others joining forces to save the world. Though the action and effects are spectacular and the villain is enjoyably menacing, the real joy of this film comes from watching ego and selfishness give way to teamwork, heroism, and selflessness.

GRADE: A

CONTENT OVERVIEW: *The Avengers* has plentiful action violence and destruction, mild language, and a mild drug reference.

MESSAGES TO DISCUSS: Strength comes from overcoming selfishness and pride to achieve unity (Doctrine and Covenants 38:27; 1 Corinthians 1:10). There is no greater love than to be willing to die for others (John 15:13). Use of force is justified to defend the innocent from tyranny and oppression (Alma 43:45–47).

BABE (G, 1995)

An award-winning box office hit, this delightful live-action family film finds a young outcast pig making a place for himself on a bustling farm by being polite, kind, and selfless. Herding sheep may be his best bet at avoiding the butcher's block. If that doesn't sound appealing to you, rest assured, this is an exceptionally charming, heartwarming keeper that'll please the whole family. Skip the sequel.

GRADE: A

CONTENT OVERVIEW: There is no sexuality, nudity, or foul language. A duck mentions trying to make eggs with the hens (in order to make himself useful and avoid being butchered). The film deals with mortality and separation; a piglet is parted from his mother, and a sheep is killed by a pack of dogs.

MESSAGES TO DISCUSS: Being kind and polite is a wonderful virtue that defuses contention (Proverbs 15:1). We ought to be kind to those who are cruel to us (Matthew 5:44).

BAMBI (G, 1942)

A seminal Disney tale about a young deer's journey from baby to full-grown buck, gaining wisdom, friendships, and lessons in mortality and romance along the way, Bambi still retains its wholesome artistry. Sweet, good-natured, and big-hearted, with gorgeous hand-drawn animation, it has earned its classic status.

GRADE: B+

CONTENT OVERVIEW: There are several scenes of intense peril, as animals flee from hunters and forest fires. That Bambi's mother dies in an off-screen shooting has, of course, broken children's hearts for generations.

MESSAGES TO DISCUSS: Children can learn vital lessons from their mothers (Alma 56:47–48). "Death is one fact that no one can escape or deny. . . . The darkness of death can ever be dispelled by the light of revealed truth. . . . This reassurance—yes, even holy confirmation—of life beyond the grave could well provide the peace promised by the Savior. . . . Those who walk with God in this earthly pilgrimage know from blessed experience that He will not abandon His children who trust in Him. In the night of death, His presence will be 'better than [a] light and safer than a known way.'" (Monson, Thomas S. "Now Is the Time," *Ensign*, Nov. 2001, 59).

BEAUTY AND THE BEAST (G, 1991)

As the first animated film to be nominated for an Academy Award for Best Picture, *Beauty and the Beast* is certainly worthy of the honor. Based on the classic fairy tale of an imprisoned woman who heals the wounded soul of a hideously transfigured prince, this romantic fable is bursting with the quality audiences expected from Disney in the early 90s. Complete with memorable characters, lush animation, good humor, and terrific music, it's great for all ages.

GRADE: A+

CONTENT OVERVIEW: There is no sexuality, vulgarity, or language. There is some violence (a villain falls to his death after battling the Beast) and threatening moments (the Beast loses his temper, roaring and shouting; the heroine is threatened by wolves; villagers storm a castle with weapons while crying "kill the Beast!")

MESSAGES TO DISCUSS: We should follow the Lord's example by looking past a person's outward appearance to consider their heart (1 Samuel 16:7). When our hearts are knit together in love, we are comforted and strong (Colossians 2:2).

BELLA (PG-13, 2006)

This unique drama, about an unwed pregnant woman befriended by a chef, is unabashedly pro-life in its message and contains positive depictions of lifelong marriage, familial loyalty, Christian faith, taking responsibility for one's choices, and the healing power of forgiveness. *Bella* is a well-acted celebration of family, charity, adoption, and Hispanic culture.

GRADE: A-

CONTENT OVERVIEW: A woman discovers that she is pregnant out of wedlock and that the father has no interest in helping to raise the child. The woman wears a tank top for much of the film. A male recounts the traumatic experience of causing a fatal car accident (a flashback accompanies the story, with mild blood), while a woman recounts the tragedy of her own father's death. A woman considers having an abortion, but (spoiler) decides against it.

MESSAGES TO DISCUSS: Faith in God can sustain us in our trials (Mosiah 24:13–15) as can the support of family and friends (Mosiah 18:8–9). Every single life is precious (Doctrine and Covenants 18:10).

BELLS OF ST. MARY'S, THE (NR, 1945)

Nominated for Best Picture, Best Actor, and Best Actress at the Academy Awards, this lovely, faith-affirming sequel to *Going My Way* once again finds Bing Crosby (*White Christmas*) as a traveling, singing, do-gooding priest named Father O'Malley. Here he teams with Ingrid Bergman (*Casablanca*), who gives a heartbreaking and heartwarming performance as a nun in charge of a dilapidated Catholic school on the verge of being shut down. Despite their differences, they become unlikely friends and allies as they try to save the school and teach the children Christian values. There's more, but I won't spoil the surprises. Suffice to say that this is the best kind of tear-jerker, uplifting and sprinkled with terrific music.

GRADE: A-

CONTENT OVERVIEW: There's no sexuality or language here. Some boys fight on the playground, with a priest saying it's good for them and a nun finding it abhorrent.

MESSAGES TO DISCUSS: It isn't what we acquire in life; it's what we give that matters (Luke 9:24, Matthew 6:20, Luke 21:1–4). Let us always be doing good and not procrastinate helping others (Alma 7:24).

BEST TWO YEARS, THE (PG, 2003)

The quintessential LDS comedy finds four missionaries sharing an apartment in Holland and enduring crises of faith, new companions, and rejection (by both investigators and girlfriends back home). Hilariously true to missionary life, with plenty of laugh-out-loud moments and a few scenes of surprising dramatic poignancy. The gorgeous on-location footage shot in Holland accentuates the experiences.

GRADE: A-

CONTENT OVERVIEW: There's nothing offensive here.

MESSAGES TO DISCUSS: Serving others can bring us comfort and joy in the midst of our own heartaches. We can know of the truthfulness of the restored gospel through prayer and the power of the Holy Ghost

(Moroni 10:3–5). Faith, hope, and charity qualify us for missionary work (Doctrine and Covenants 4).

BETWEEN HEAVEN AND EARTH (NR, 2002)

This is an inspiring and informative film, produced by the Church, about the history and importance of temples. The film benefits tremendously by interviewing General Authorities, secular historians, and theologians of other faiths, offering a thorough understanding of temples in biblical and modern times. For those who are preparing to enter the temple or those who'd like to enrich their experiences in the house of the Lord, this film is a must.

GRADE: B

CONTENT OVERVIEW: There's nothing offensive here.

MESSAGES TO DISCUSS: The temple is the house of the Lord (John 2:16; Luke 19:46). It is sacred (1 Kings 9:3; 2 Chronicles 30:8); therefore, only those who have prepared themselves are worthy to enter (Psalm 24:3–4; 2 Chronicles 23:19).

BEYOND THE GATES OF SPLENDOR (PG-13, 2002)

This handsomely made documentary portrays the true story of a group of Christian missionaries who were murdered by natives in the jungles of Ecuador and how that led to the end of centuries of tribal warfare as killers converted to Christ through the forgiveness and service of the missionaries' families. In addition to being a powerful real-world reminder of the power of Christ and His doctrine, the film is also a wonderful exploration of intercultural relations and friendships. In 2005 the filmmakers made a wonderful drama based on these events entitled *End of the Spear.*

GRADE: A

CONTENT OVERVIEW: Some natives are shown in the nude in archival footage, though the context is hardly sexual or inappropriate (think *National Geographic*). There's no language, but accounts of warfare and murder are described in somewhat graphic detail—there are photographs of the dead missionaries and dramatizations show persons stabbed with spears.

MESSAGES TO DISCUSS: Healing can come from loving our enemies and doing good to them that have wronged us (Matthew 5:43–44). We are commanded to forgive one another (Doctrine and Covenants 64:10–11). Even the most vicious of people can be changed through faith in Jesus Christ (Alma 24:16–19).

BIG MIRACLE (PG, 2012)

Based on the true story of Operation Breakthrough, the 1988 attempt to rescue three gray whales trapped in the Alaskan ice, *Big Miracle* is an intelligent and uplifting family movie. Though some characters are a bit one dimensional and there's little spark between John Krasinski (TV's *The Office*) and Drew Barrymore (*Ever After*) as they inch toward reconciliation as a former couple, all of the performances are fun, and the history is fascinating. The film's greatest strength is how it captures, in such a refreshingly human and entertaining way, the complex dynamics among an oil tycoon seeking good PR, an environmentalist trying to make a point, a journalist sensing a career opportunity, Reagan-era politicos looking for votes, and Inupiat whale hunters seeking to be left alone. That these very different people with very different motivations ultimately unite with one noble goal is to be expected, but the acting, writing, and filmmaking make it satisfying nonetheless.

GRADE: B

CONTENT OVERVIEW: There is some mild profanity, but no violence or sexuality.

MESSAGES TO DISCUSS: Whales, like all living creatures, are the marvelous creations of God (Genesis 1:21; Moses 2:21; Abraham 4:21). We should strive to eliminate contention and to increase unity, understanding, and love with one another (Mosiah 18:21).

BLIND SIDE, THE (PG-13, 2009)

This moving and well-acted drama based on a true story finds Sandra Bullock and Tim McGraw as a well-to-do Southern couple who take in an African-American teen from a drug-and-gang-infested neighborhood and make him part of the family. It is warm and inspiring, with an Oscar-winning performance by Bullock.

GRADE: B+

CONTENT OVERVIEW: There are a few moderate profanities, a scene of violence (an ugly brawl in a tough neighborhood), and a mother jokes that if her adopted son impregnates a girl out of wedlock, she'll castrate him.

MESSAGES TO DISCUSS: Those with riches should use them to clothe the naked and feed the hungry (Jacob 2:18–19). All of us, regardless of race, are brothers and sisters, children of God (2 Nephi 26:33).

BOLT (PG, 2008)

Bolt is a charming and touching Disney animated film about a television-star dog who thinks he has superpowers and his quest to rescue his master, a girl who he believes has been kidnapped (he's wrong on both counts). Teaming up with a sly feline and a ready-for-action hamster, he sets out across the country to find her. It has nice vocal work, impressive animation, and a finale that'll move you to tears.

GRADE: B+

CONTENT OVERVIEW: There are several scenes of children and animals in peril, as well as moments (scripted for a television show) of vehicular mayhem and explosions.

MESSAGES TO DISCUSS: There is no greater love than to be willing to die for another (John 15:13). The truth frees us to live without delusion and to reach our true potential (John 8:32).

BRAVE (PG, 2012)

It borrows too heavily from *Brother Bear*, but Disney-Pixar's *Brave* is ultimately redeemed by stunning animation, a gorgeous musical score, excellent characters, rough-and-tumble humor, and an undeniably powerful emotional core. The story finds Merida, a strong-willed and feisty Scottish princess, at odds with her mother over her betrothal. With the unification of warring clans at stake, the two come to understand each other after a witches' curse forces them to work together.

GRADE: B+

CONTENT OVERVIEW: Disney-Pixar's *Brave* contains some fairly intense scenes of peril that could frighten children, comedic brawling and fisticuffs, and humorous animated rear nudity of adult males and toddlers. A heavyset female character is portrayed with ample cleavage, again for comedic effect.

MESSAGES TO DISCUSS:

"Mothers, take time to be a real friend to your children. Listen to your children, really listen. Talk with them, laugh and joke with them, sing with them, play with them, cry with them, hug them, honestly praise them" (Ezra Taft Benson, "News of the Church," *Ensign*, May 1987).

> Arguments, fights . . . generation gaps . . . all fall into this category of pride. Contention in our families drives the Spirit of the Lord away. It also drives many of our family members away. . . . Pride adversely affects all our relationships. . . . God will have a humble people. Either we can choose to be humble or we can be compelled to be humble. . . . Let us choose to be humble. We can choose to humble ourselves by conquering enmity toward our brothers and sisters, esteeming them as ourselves, and lifting them as high as or higher than we are. We can

choose to humble ourselves by receiving counsel and chastisement. We can choose to humble ourselves by forgiving those who have offended us. (Ezra Taft Benson, "Beware of Pride," *Ensign,* May 1989)

BRIAN REGAN:

EPITOME OF HYPERBOLE (NR, 2008)
STANDING UP (NR, 2007)
I WALKED ON THE MOON (NR, 2004)

Squeaky clean stand-up comedian Brian Regan, by now a legend in many LDS circles, brings his trademark wit and expressive physicality to the stage in these three separate comedy specials. One of the funniest (and most successful) stand-up acts in the business, Regan is all the more impressive because he doesn't rely on vulgarity. All three are terrific, but *I Walked on the Moon* is the best if you must choose just one.

GRADE: A

CONTENT OVERVIEW: A few mild profanities, but no harsh language and no sexual humor.

MESSAGES TO DISCUSS: "In all of living have much fun and laughter. Life is to be enjoyed, not just endured" (Gordon B. Hinckley, "Stand True and Faithful," *Ensign,* May 1996).

BRIGHAM CITY (PG-13, 2001)

Writer-director Richard Dutcher's underrated "Mormon murder mystery" finds a small Utah town terrorized by a serial killer. It's well-acted and highly accessible to audiences not of our faith, using the culture and religion not to convert audiences, but to flavor the story. Dutcher tastefully (and effectively) leaves most of the violence to our imagination. In its examination of a once-peaceful small town torn apart by fear and mistrust, it feels totally real, making it truly scary and profoundly moving. Really a spiritual drama masquerading as a scary movie, what sets *Brigham City* apart is its focus on the role of faith and community in healing the deepest emotional and spiritual wounds.

GRADE: A-

CONTENT OVERVIEW: *Brigham City* has no language or sexuality. Several people are murdered off screen, though there are intense moments building up to the killings, as well as a few somewhat graphic images (bloody photos of the deceased). It is stated that a victim was raped before she was killed. An engaged man and woman mention "saving themselves for their wedding night."

MESSAGES TO DISCUSS: We should not partake of the sacrament unworthily (Mormon 9:29). Beware of deceivers, wolves in sheep's clothing (Matthew 7:15). In order for us to be forgiven and find peace, we must forgive others (Matthew 6:14–15).

BUG'S LIFE, A (G, 1998)

An oft-overlooked entry in Disney-Pixar's canon, this tale of an ant who enlists a group of circus-performing insects to protect his colony from grasshoppers is a charming and heartwarming film that deserves to be revisited. Taking its cues from *Seven Samurai*, *The Magnificent Seven*, and *Three Amigos*, this is a cleverly written, laugh-out-loud romp for the whole family.

GRADE: A-

CONTENT OVERVIEW: There is no language or sexuality. An insect asks a male ladybug if he'd like to "pollinate with a real bug" (the insect thinks the ladybug is a female). In the "outtakes" there is a flatulence gag. A villain is eaten by a bird. A flea is engulfed in an explosion (no harm comes to him other than appearing "smoked").

MESSAGES TO DISCUSS: All secrets come out sooner or later (2 Nephi 30:17). There is great strength in standing united (Psalms 133:1; 3 Nephi 27:1; Doctrine and Covenants 107:27).

CALLED TO SERVE (NR, UNKNOWN RELEASE YEAR)

This classic thirty-minute documentary, produced by the Church, gives audiences a glimpse into missionary life, from the openings of mission calls to learning foreign languages in the MTC to serving in the field. Though the fashions and hairstyles add to the fun (it appears to have been filmed in the 1980s), this is ultimately a powerfully spiritual short film that has inspired several generations to share the gospel as full-time missionaries.

GRADE: B+

CONTENT OVERVIEW: There is nothing offensive here.

MESSAGES TO DISCUSS: The field is white, ready to harvest; serve God with all your heart, mind, and strength; serve humanity with hope, charity, and love (Doctrine and Covenants 4). The gospel will be preached to everyone in their own language (Doctrine and Covenants 90:11).

CAPTAIN AMERICA: THE FIRST AVENGER (PG-13, 2011)

Clichéd as a superhero origin tale, but rollicking as a patriotic crowd-pleaser, this WWII Marvel Comics actioneer may stumble over its more cartoonish elements, but it boasts excellent stunts, deft wit, good romance, and fine performances all around. Chris Evans impresses with earnest humility as a weakling transformed into a super-soldier, Hayley Atwell brings class and spunk as his love interest, Hugo Weaving hams it up enjoyably as an evil German, Stanley Tucci exudes paternal warmth, and Tommy Lee Jones hasn't been this fun in years.

GRADE: B

CONTENT OVERVIEW: *Captain America* has plenty of bloodless war violence and fighting, with one incident of quick blood spray. Language is minimal, with only a few mild (and one moderate) uses of profanity. Some characters drink alcohol. A villain kills unarmed persons. There is no nudity or sexuality apart from two kisses.

MESSAGES TO DISCUSS: True heroes do not enjoy violence or killing, but they will forcefully defend liberty and innocent lives if necessary, even to the point of giving up their own lives (Alma 48:11–14).

CARS (G, 2006)

I initially viewed *Cars* as a lesser Pixar film, a vehicle (if you'll pardon the expression) for selling toys with a fluffy story. With time, however, I've succumbed to its folksy, old-fashioned Americana charm and its variety of memorable characters. This is a warm and worthwhile tale of an arrogant hotshot racecar who learns humility, altruism, and charity while stuck in a small town on Route 66. The animation is alternately flashy and lovely depending on the situation, and the vocal work is terrific. Kids may enjoy the soulless sequel, but adults will most appreciate this heartwarming original.

GRADE: A

CONTENT OVERVIEW: There is no foul language or sexuality. A female car has a tattoo on her backside. Nascar-style races feature crashes, with anthropomorphized cars banged up (but none killed).

MESSAGES TO DISCUSS: We are to love our neighbors as ourselves, putting their needs before our own (Galatians 5:14). The proud will be made humble, whereas humility leads to the kind of success that matters (Luke 14:11; Philippians 2:3).

CASABLANCA (PG, 1942)

World War II love story (filmed while WWII was actually going on) earns its status as one of cinema's all-time great romances. Humphrey Bogart stars as a nightclub owner in the Arabian city of Casablanca, fleeing from the war and his own broken heart. Both arrive on his doorstep when his ex-lover (Ingrid Bergman) and her presumed-dead husband walk into his club, forcing him to choose between love and virtue. A timeless tale of morality amid heartache, with iconic dialogue and terrific performances, *Casablanca* is a must-see for every movie fan.

GRADE: A+

CONTENT OVERVIEW: There are three bloodless shootings, some drinking and smoking, and a few mild profanities.

MESSAGES TO DISCUSS: Spouses are to remain faithful to each other (Doctrine and Covenants 42:22). Righteousness involves putting others before ourselves (Philippians 2:3).

CHARIOTS OF FIRE (PG, 1981)

One of the most spiritually nourishing films ever made, this Best Picture winner tells the true story of two runners, a Jew and a Christian, who compete in the 1924 Olympics. The former faces persecution, the latter is pressured to compromise his values for the "good of the country." How each of them deals with their trials will inspire viewers to more fully commit to serving the Lord and magnifying their talents. Though it can be dry in parts, its flaws are more than made up for by the solid acting, an iconic score by Vangelis, and the powerful story.

GRADE: A-

CONTENT OVERVIEW: There is a very brief shot of a male's rear in the shower, and a woman wears a low-cut dress. There's one moderate profanity and some smoking and drinking.

MESSAGES TO DISCUSS: The Sabbath day is a holy day and is meant to be honored by refraining from work and focusing on the Lord (Exodus 20:8–11). We may experience pressure from people in power to compromise our values and covenants; only faith, truth, and prayer, along with commitment to keeping the commandments, can keep us steady on the right path (Ephesians 6:12–18). Those who honor the Lord will be honored by Him (1 Samuel 2:30).

CHARLIE AND THE CHOCOLATE FACTORY (PG, 2005)

Unfairly maligned and placed in the shadow of the Gene Wilder classic *Willy Wonka and the Chocolate Factory*, this Tim Burton-directed, Johnny Depp-starring version has a delightfully weird energy all its own. If your kids like it, it may grow on you with repeat viewings. Based on the Roald Dahl novel.

GRADE: B

CONTENT OVERVIEW: There is one mild profanity, one instance of a woman drinking, and several instances of children in apparent peril.

MESSAGES TO DISCUSS: Parents should treat their children with tenderness, teach them right and wrong, (1 Nephi 8:37) and support them in pursuing their dreams. Nothing is as precious as family (*The*

Family—a Proclamation to the World). We shouldn't waste time in fruitless pursuits (Doctrine and Covenants 60:13), such as overuse of media. Don't be a glutton (Proverbs 23:2–12).

CHARLIE BROWN CHRISTMAS, A (TV-G, 1965)

This classic is an annual must-watch for many families, as the *Peanuts* gang unites to celebrate the true meaning of Christmas. It's funny and has terrific music.

GRADE: A+

CONTENT OVERVIEW: Some of the children are sarcastic to one another but ultimately learn to show love and friendship.

MESSAGES TO DISCUSS: The birth of Christ our Savior provides the real meaning of Christmas (Matthew 1:18–25; Matthew 2; Luke 1; Luke 2). Our potential is more likely to be met if we are loved.

CHARLIE BROWN THANKSGIVING, A (TV-G, 1973)

The *Peanuts* gang celebrates Thanksgiving in this animated classic, as Peppermint Patty invites herself and her friends over to Charlie Brown's home for Thanksgiving and the kids learn about the history behind the holiday. It features laughs aplenty and iconic characters.

GRADE: B

CONTENT OVERVIEW: Some of the children are sarcastic to one another but ultimately learn to show love and friendship.

MESSAGES TO DISCUSS: It is wrong to act entitled and spoiled, not working for what we receive (2 Thessalonians 3:10). The Pilgrims were guided to the Americas by the hand of the Lord (1 Nephi 13:12–19)

CHARLY (PG, 2002)

The quintessential LDS romantic film, *Charly* retains everything audiences love about the story and characters from Jack Weyland's novel. This story of a free-spirited New Yorker who falls for a straight-laced Mormon man tends to be melodramatic but, when all is said and done, Heather Beers and Jeremy Hoop have wonderful chemistry, and Charly remains a compelling firecracker of a character. The humor mostly hits the mark, and the film is undeniably effective as a tearjerker and as a testimony of both eternal marriage and the peace found through Jesus Christ.

GRADE: B

CONTENT OVERVIEW: There are some very mild comedic innuendos and frank discussions about chastity.

MESSAGES TO DISCUSS: Though all die, through Christ all will live again (1 Corinthians 15:22). Marriage was meant to be eternal (1 Corinthians 11:11; Doctrine and Covenants 132:19–20). The Lord is merciful to those who sin in ignorance, so we ought to be as well (Mosiah 3:11).

CHITTY CHITTY BANG BANG (G, 1968)

This delightful tale of an inventor, his two children, the woman he falls for, and a flying car is bursting with imagination, creativity, and engaging song-and-dance numbers (the title song, "Truly Scrumptious," and "Toot-Sweet" are particular highlights.) At two hours and twenty minutes in length, it's overlong for this type of film, but it's fun, and Dick Van Dyke is excellent as always.

GRADE: B+

CONTENT OVERVIEW: A "child catcher" imprisons and threatens to kill children (he's not successful).

MESSAGES TO DISCUSS: Imagination can add flavor and fun to life. Beware those who flatter and offer pleasures (2 Nephi 28:21).

CHRISTMAS ORANGES (PG, 2012)

The famous tale of kindness among lonely children at an orphanage is brought to life in *Christmas Oranges*, the most accomplished film yet from LDS director John Lyde. It has some terrific performances, from the gruff, Scrooge-like headmaster played by Edward Herrmann

(*Redemption*) to the warmth displayed by Nancy Stafford (*Matlock, Christmas With a Capitol C*); from some terrifically nuanced work by LDS film veteran Bruce Newbold (*Finding Faith in Christ, Only a Stonecutter*) to solid acting by the children led by Bailee Michelle Johnson (*17 Miracles*). This is a beautiful Christmas film with a timeless message. It is lovingly crafted, well-acted, and told with warmth and tenderness.

GRADE: B+

CONTENT OVERVIEW: Some children bully others. Some children get sick and pass away, as does a beloved adult.

MESSAGES TO DISCUSS: Kindness can melt stubborn and cold hearts. "Let us not complain at our friends and neighbors, because they do not do what we want them to do. Rather let us love them into doing the things our Heavenly Father would have them do. We can do that, and we cannot win their confidence or their love in any other way" (George Albert Smith, Conference Report, October 1945, 174). Charity means putting others' needs first (Alma 15:18).

CHRISTMAS WITH A CAPITAL C (PG, 2011)

Christmas with a Capital C uses a small Alaskan town as the setting to explore the culture war between secularism and Christianity. Although it admittedly struggles with some ham-fisted storytelling and "cheesy" characterization for its first half, to its enormous credit, it gains traction as it transcends initial "us versus them" arguments to examine the real-world value of the Savior's command that we love our enemies instead of judging them. The characters learn to recognize that our commitment to Him should be manifest in our actions and attitudes, not just our bumper stickers. Once it fleshes out the characters, this film actually becomes quite moving, and its beauty is only bolstered by the lovely Alaskan scenery.

GRADE: B-

CONTENT OVERVIEW: There is no offensive content here.

MESSAGES TO DISCUSS: Don't be ashamed to witness Christ to the world (Romans 1:16). "Who am I to judge another when I walk imperfectly? In the quiet heart is hidden sorrow that the eye can't see. Who am I to judge another? Lord, I would follow thee" ("Lord, I Would Follow Thee," *Hymns*, no. 220).

CHRONICLES OF NARNIA, THE: THE LION, THE WITCH, AND THE WARDROBE (PG, 2005)

This big-budget Disney adaptation is faithful to the classic C. S. Lewis novel. The story is rich with Christian allegory concerning the Atonement, the Resurrection, the battle of Armageddon, faith, obedience, and repentance. All these topics are dealt with in a manner that is both easily understood by children and profoundly moving for adults. Imaginative storytelling and great special effects are among the highlights as four British children from the World War II–era step through a wardrobe into a mystical land where the righteous lion Aslan does battle with the evil White Witch.

GRADE: B+

CONTENT OVERVIEW: There is some fantasy battle violence and intense moments where people and animals are in peril. Recommended for older children and up.

MESSAGES TO DISCUSS: Like the White Witch and her Turkish Delight, Satan will use pleasure to tempt us to betray what's right (2 Nephi 28:21). Like Aslan, Jesus Christ gave his life to pay the price of our mistakes, then returned to life to allow others to do the same (Mosiah 3:7–10). As in the film, good will face off with evil in a final battle (Revelations 16:14–16; Doctrine and Covenants 45:48–52, 55).

CHRONICLES OF NARNIA, THE: PRINCE CASPIAN (PG, 2008)

This second film based on C. S. Lewis fantasy novels finds the Pevensie siblings returning to Narnia to help a righteous prince overthrow a wicked pretender to the throne. Grittier and less magical than the film that preceded it (much like *The Two Towers* was to the *Fellowship of the Ring*), this is still a powerful tale with gospel messages weaved throughout. The epic battles and intense moments probably should have qualified this as PG-13, but it's still marvelous storytelling for older children, teens, and adults.

GRADE: B

CONTENT OVERVIEW: There is some intense battle violence, with people and animals killed in combat.

MESSAGES TO DISCUSS: Perhaps, instead of seeking proof from God, we need to prove ourselves to him (Ether 12:6). Pride can make us easily distracted, easily tempted, easily divided, and unprepared to meet God (Doctrine and Covenants 23:1; Alma 5:28).

CHRONICLES OF NARNIA, THE: THE VOYAGE OF THE DAWN TREADER (PG, 2010)

This third Narnia film, *The Chronicles of Narnia: The Voyage of the Dawn Treader*, is in many ways the most satisfying entry in the series. Two of the Pevensie children return to Narnia with their duplicitous cousin and hitch a ride aboard the Prince's ship in this seafaring adventure to find Caspian's father's advisors. After a somewhat clunky start, the film ultimately develops the relationships between new and returning characters in moving and dramatically satisfying ways. Complete with merfolk, pirates, and dragons, it also features some terrific action, especially toward the end. The acting and digital effects are better than they've ever been.

GRADE: B

CONTENT OVERVIEW: There are some intense moments and startling images in this PG film, including a battle with a sea creature and against a band of warriors. There is no language or sexuality.

MESSAGES TO DISCUSS: The proud will be humbled, while the humble will be exalted (Luke 14:11). Pride makes us susceptible to temptation (Doctrine and Covenants 23:1), whereas humility and faith help us to overcome it (Doctrine and Covenants 10:5).

CINDERELLA (G, 1950)

This classic Disney cartoon is one of their romantic greats, with lonely orphan Cinderella in servitude to her wicked stepmother and cruel stepsisters until an encounter with a fairy godmother and a handsome prince change her destiny. The love story is fine, but it's the peripheral characters, including some hilarious mice, that give the film its kick.

GRADE: B+

CONTENT OVERVIEW: There is nothing offensive here.

MESSAGES TO DISCUSS: You reap what you sow; kindness is ultimately rewarded (Doctrine and Covenants 6:33), while cruel people will get what they deserve (Job 4:8).

CITY LIGHTS (G, 1931)

City Lights is Charlie Chaplin's best film. This silent comedy masterpiece has some terrific physical comedy, but it's the tender romance that'll bring tears to your eyes as Chaplin's homeless transient endures humiliation and hardship to help a blind flower girl. That he wants to help her out of pure charity, regardless of whether she ever loves him back, is what makes this such a unique and wonderful love story. It's also gut-bustingly funny; a scene in which Chaplin faces a boxer twice his size is one of his finest moments.

GRADE: A+

CONTENT OVERVIEW: Two characters repeatedly get drunk. Some punches are thrown in a boxing scene, but it's played for laughs.

MESSAGES TO DISCUSS: When we love someone, we put his or her needs before our own, even if that means we suffer for his or her benefit (Moroni 7:45).

CLOUDY WITH A CHANCE OF MEATBALLS (PG, 2009)

This tale of a young inventor who, desperate for fatherly approval, makes it rain food in his hometown, will delight children and adults with its memorable characters, creative visuals, and hilarious non-sequiturs. One of the most entertaining family movies in years, yet sadly it's often overlooked. Based on the children's book with the same name.

GRADE: A-

CONTENT OVERVIEW: There is some slapstick violence and scenes of peril.

MESSAGES TO DISCUSS: We all have different gifts and talents; we need to accept one another and encourage each other to develop our skills (Romans 12:3–9).

CONSPIRATOR, THE (PG-13, 2010)

Directed by Robert Redford, *The Conspirator* tells of a young Union attorney who defends a Southern mother charged with aiding and abetting those who murdered Abraham Lincoln. His disdain for the woman turns to compassion and outrage as constitutional rights are trampled on by a prosecution intent on blind vengeance. It's a well-written, well-acted historical drama with plenty of modern parallels, which makes up for the occasional times when it's a bit too slowly paced and heavy-handed. A soul-stirring, troubling, and thought-provoking examination of the sacred and true nature of the Constitution, it's also a warning against allowing fear to cause us to abandon our freedom in pursuit of security.

GRADE: B+

CONTENT OVERVIEW: Portrays the Lincoln assassination and the attempted murder of the Secretary of State, the former by shooting and the latter by stabbing. Both are bloodless but intense moments. There is some moderate language early on in response to the horrific events. Criminals are placed in hoods and executed by hanging. There is no sexuality or nudity.

MESSAGES TO DISCUSS: The United States Constitution is an inspired document (Doctrine and Covenants 101:76–80). Real character comes from doing what is right, in spite of opposition and great personal cost (Job 1; 2 Nephi 2:11–13). Lust for revenge can cloud the pursuit of true justice (Romans 12:19; Doctrine and Covenants 64:9–11).

COOL RUNNINGS (PG, 1993)

Loosely based on the true story of athletes from the tropical nation of Jamaica competing as bobsledders in the 1988 Winter Olympics, this is one of my favorite Disney comedies. This is a delightfully funny live-action movie with memorable characters and a surprisingly moving ending.

GRADE: B+

CONTENT OVERVIEW: There is some drinking, a few mild profanities, mention of a girl accidentally seeing a boy's "ding-a-ling," and a bar-room brawl.

MESSAGES TO DISCUSS: Hard work is rewarded (2 Chronicles 15:7); some things can only be accomplished by getting along and working as a team (2 Nephi 1:21).

CORALINE (PG, 2009)

Like the morbid tales penned by the Brothers' Grimm, *Coraline* is a creepy morality tale that won't appeal to everyone. This stop-motion wonder from director Henry Selick (*The Nightmare Before Christmas, James and the Giant Peach*) is a triumph of creative artistry and dazzling animation. It tells the story of the titular heroine, a plucky and resourceful girl with apathetic parents, who stumbles into what appears to be a parallel version of her life where everything is exactly as she wishes it were in reality. The dreariness of her true home is replaced by vibrant colors and spectacle. Her neglectful parents are replaced by updated versions who live only to lavish her with affection and wish-fulfillment. It's all seems perfect, but she (and the audience) cannot shake the unsettling suspicion that something isn't quite right. Only a sage old black cat seems to understand the dangers behind the seductive façade of Coraline's dream world. A terrific cautionary tale whose themes parallel the eternal principle that following the Lord and His prophets is better than succumbing to the binding temptations of the adversary.

GRADE: A-

CONTENT OVERVIEW: While the film contains no real violence, it is full of unsettling images and a creepy atmosphere that will doubtless give nightmares to little ones (much like the wicked witch from *The Wizard of Oz*). There is mild profanity and an immodestly dressed and buxom elderly woman; though a clay-animated figure and far from titillating, it may be offensive to some.

MESSAGES TO DISCUSS: Beware the flattering words of those who tell you what you want to hear and offer to give you what you want but are actually trying to harm you (2 Nephi 28:22). Heed the warnings of those who know (Doctrine and Covenants 1:4).

CORPSE BRIDE (PG, 2005)

Tim Burton's stop-motion-animated film is perfectly cast with Johnny Depp voicing a betrothed young man who runs from his wedding and meets a deceased woman (Helena Bonham Carter) who wants him as her own. Funny and imaginative with some dazzling art direction and terrific songs, this one is perfect for the Halloween season.

GRADE: B+

CONTENT OVERVIEW: There is a sword duel and plenty of macabre, non-graphic physical humor.

MESSAGES TO DISCUSS:: The wicked receive their just desserts (Job 4:8). In seeking our own happiness, we must be careful to not deprive others of theirs (Philippians 2:4).

COURAGEOUS (PG-13, 2011)

This Christian drama uses the form of a police thriller to thoroughly and poignantly explore the need for strong, loving, and faithful fathers and husbands. While moments of genuine dramatic power are diluted somewhat by distracting melodrama, amateur acting, and broad humor, there's also some truly terrific stuff here. The virtues of integrity, altruism, love, and bravery are portrayed in a manner that makes them attainable and practical. As a call to action and as an invitation to come unto Christ, *Courageous* packs plenty of spiritual firepower against the forces of error that are dragging men, and their families, down into despair and sin.

GRADE: B+

CONTENT OVERVIEW: *Courageous* is rated PG-13, but it's a very mild PG-13. The police engage in shootouts and fistfights with criminals, but the emphasis is on heroism, bravery, and protecting the innocent, not on glorifying violence. It feels more like a PG-rated film, with no foul language, gore, or sexuality. The rating comes simply from the presence of drugs in criminal possession, but in this regard, and all others, evil is portrayed only to contrast it with good.

MESSAGES TO DISCUSS: The Lord would have us serve Him by visiting and helping those who are sick, naked, hungry, or in prison (Matthew 25:34–40).

By the way you love her mother, you will teach your daughter about tenderness, loyalty, respect, compassion, and devotion. She will learn from your example what to expect from young men and what qualities to seek in a future spouse. You can show your daughter by they way you love and honor your wife that she should never settle for less. Your example will teach your daughter to value womanhood. You are showing her that she is a daughter of our Heavenly Father, who loves her. (Elaine S. Dalton, "Love Her Mother," *Ensign*, Nov. 2011)

Teach your children about Christ and lead them to rejoice in Him, so they may know how to have their sins washed away through His grace (2 Nephi 25:23, 26).

"Fatherhood is leadership, the most important kind of leadership. It has always been so; it always will be so. . . . The title *father* is sacred and eternal. It is significant that of all the titles of respect and honor and admiration given to Deity, He has asked us to address Him as Father" (Quorum of the Twelve Apostles, "Father, Consider Your Ways," *Ensign*, June 2002).

COURT JESTER, THE (G, 1955)

The great Danny Kaye, so amusing in *White Christmas*, stars in one of my all-time favorite comedies, *The Court Jester*, about a medieval entertainer-turned-spy who infiltrates a castle to overthrow an oppressive king. This is a brilliant showcase for Kaye, who proves himself a master of catchy music, pithy one-liners, athletic physical comedy, and terrific tongue twisters. I cannot recommend it enough.

GRADE: A+

CONTENT OVERVIEW: There are a few mild innuendos (it was made in the 1950s, so nothing crass) and some battles with swords, bows, and arrows.

MESSAGES TO DISCUSS: Being tender and nurturing doesn't negate masculinity, it enhances it (2 Timothy 2:24; Alma 7:23). Be strong and of a good courage in resisting evil (Deuteronomy 31:6).

DESPICABLE ME (PG, 2010)

This surprise hit animated film finds a super-villain (Steve Carell) undergoing a change of heart when his plans for world domination are interrupted by the arrival of three sweet orphan girls. The story is warm-hearted and very funny. And the "minions" are brilliant.

GRADE: A-

CONTENT OVERVIEW: Some slapstick violence and mild vulgarity.

MESSAGES TO DISCUSS: No matter who you are or what you've done, it's never too late to change and do the right thing (Alma 26:17–22).

DINOSAUR (PG, 2000)

Groundbreaking special effects highlight this Disney tale of a herd of dinosaurs and monkeys in search of a new home after an asteroid hits. The storytelling is too formulaic to appeal much to adults, but kids will love it.

GRADE: B-

CONTENT OVERVIEW: There are some tense moments as predatory dinosaurs attack other dinosaurs and animals flee the explosive effects of an asteroid crash. Male and female monkeys discuss finding a mate, then, having done so, swing into the night on vines in pairs.

MESSAGES TO DISCUSS: The Lord meant for all creatures to join, male and female, to multiply and replenish the earth (Moses 2:20–25). There is great strength in standing united (Psalms 133:1; 3 Nephi 27:1; Doctrine and Covenants 107:27).

DRAGONHEART (PG-13, 1996)

Sean Connery gives voice to Draco, the last surviving dragon who forms an unlikely alliance with a dragonslayer (Dennis Quaid) to overthrow an evil king in this combination of live-action and CGI. The characters are underdeveloped and it borrows heavily from other films, but the action is great, the music is phenomenal, and the special effects still impress. Older kids and fantasy-loving teens will enjoy it.

GRADE: B-

CONTENT OVERVIEW: There are a few mild profanities, plenty of battle violence (people killed with swords and arrows, etc.), and a brief creepy scene with an evil king attempting to seduce a woman, kissing her against her will, but she pulls a knife on him and escapes.

MESSAGES TO DISCUSS: With forgiveness and understanding, our enemies can become our friends (Alma 26:29–31).

DUMBO (G, 1941)

This Disney classic finds a young elephant with oversized ears transformed, by the love of his mother and the friendship of a mouse, from circus laughingstock to circus hero. Unforgettable characters and musical numbers make this a treat for all ages.

GRADE: A

CONTENT OVERVIEW: Dumbo and Timothy the mouse accidentally get drunk leading them to hallucinate about "pink elephants on parade." Several crows smoke cigars.

MESSAGES TO DISCUSS: More important than outward appearance is one's heart and character (1 Samuel 16:7). The Lord commands us to not gossip (1 Timothy 5:13; Doctrine and Covenants 42:27; Doctrine and Covenants 88:124). Few things are as influential as a mother's love (Alma 56:47; Alma 57:21).

EARTH (G, 2007)

The Hollywood machine, capable as it is of producing fantastic tales and likable heroes, cannot touch the raw power of creation. This film is a ninety-minute version of the incredible BBC documentary miniseries *Planet Earth,* and what the film version lacks in the miniseries's thoroughness, it makes up for in a breathless pace that relentlessly transports you all over the world (as any great adventure film should). The footage is, quite simply, some of the most stunning ever captured on film, in any genre. What's more, *Earth* works as a riveting drama, following three families (polar bears, humpback whales, and African elephants) as they try to survive predators, climate change, and the search for food, over the course of one year. I found myself invested in the survival of these animals as much or more than any fictional character, due at least in part to clever editing and skillful narration by James Earl Jones. The struggles, failures, and triumphs of the Lord's creations on His canvas makes for a terrific blockbuster.

GRADE: A-

CONTENT OVERVIEW: There are some moments of animals in peril and some scenes of animals being attacked by predators, though thankfully there is no gory or bloody footage.

MESSAGES TO DISCUSS: The earth is full of the rich creations of God (Psalm 104:24).

ELLA ENCHANTED (PG, 2004)

Energetic song-and-dance numbers highlight this modernized fairy tale, based on the book about a medieval maiden cursed to obey every command given to her. As the main character, Anne Hathaway charms, as does Hugh Darcy as her princely beau. Cary Elwes, after playing the hero in *The Princess Bride*, returns to medieval fantasy-comedy here, camping it up to memorable effect as a dastardly villain.

GRADE: B+

CONTENT OVERVIEW: There are a few mild innuendos and obscenities, some threatening moments, and an ogre shows some "rear crack," but nothing here pushes the PG rating.

MESSAGES TO DISCUSS: In order for us to be happy, we must have freedom of choice and use it well (2 Nephi 2:25–28).

ELF (PG, 2003)

An instant Christmas classic upon its release, *Elf* takes the comedic talents of Will Ferrell and places them in a clean holiday comedy to such memorable effect that I know many families who watch it every year. Ferrell stars as a giant man-child, raised since infancy at the North Pole, who leaves Santa's workshop and sets out to New York to find his biological father. Very clever with belly laughs aplenty.

GRADE: A

CONTENT OVERVIEW: A man mistakes a little person for an elf, causing the little person to tackle and punch him (played for laughs). A man naively sends his father lingerie for Christmas. He takes off his tights while changing clothes as his stepmother walks in and screams (we see nothing). A woman sings in the shower; we see her from the shoulders-up. It is implied that a man fathered a son out of wedlock and is now getting to know him.

MESSAGES TO DISCUSS: When we love someone, we put his or her needs before our own, even if that means we suffer for his or her benefit (Moroni 7:45). Children deserve love and guidance from their fathers (Proverbs 4:1–10).

EMMA SMITH: MY STORY (PG, 2008)

Produced by the Joseph Smith Jr. and Emma Hale Smith Historical Society, this lushly shot and very well-acted take on the life of Emma Smith was directed by Gary Cook and T. C. Christensen, who together also directed the current Temple Square film, *Joseph Smith: The Prophet of the Restoration*. This film uses the same actors and truly feels like a companion film. Nathan Mitchell continues to impress as Brother Joseph, but it is Katherine Nelson and Patricia Place, as the younger and elder Emma respectively, who truly shine in this even-handed examination of the life, faith, and trials of this oft-misunderstood "elect lady." The film strengthens the audience's faith in the Restoration even as it tactfully deals with such subjects as plural marriage and Emma's staying behind when the Saints went to Utah. Solid production values add to the professional feel. Don't miss it.

GRADE: A

CONTENT OVERVIEW: There is nothing offensive here.

MESSAGES TO DISCUSS: Emma Smith was a chosen and elect lady, called to bless and comfort her husband, expound scripture, and select hymns (Doctrine and Covenants 25). Plural marriage was a trial, but it was also a blessing and a commandment from the Lord (Doctrine and Covenants 132:51–56)

EMPEROR'S NEW GROOVE, THE (G, 2000)

The Emperor's New Groove gets my vote for funniest Disney animated film (apologies to the excellent *Aladdin*); this is also one of my all-time favorite comedies, period. Self-absorbed Central American emperor

Kuzco learns altruism after he's overthrown, turned into a llama, and befriended by a humble peasant. Dazzling one-liners, inspired silliness, and madcap energy highlight this excellent family film.

GRADE: A+

CONTENT OVERVIEW: There are several humorous assassination attempts on Emperor Kuzco and some comedic slapstick violence and moments of peril.

MESSAGES TO DISCUSS: Happiness comes from putting the needs of others before our own (Philippians 2:4).

ENCHANTED (PG, 2007)

Enchanted features a star-making performance by Amy Adams as an animated Disney princess who's banished to the live-action world, where she finds her notions of love challenged by life's harsh realities when she falls for a divorce lawyer. A brilliant thesis on fairy-tale romance versus the real thing, this is a clever, funny, and ultimately uplifting film with terrific music. Patrick Dempsey, Susan Sarandon, and James Marsden give excellent supporting performances.

GRADE: A

CONTENT OVERVIEW: There's a few mild obscenities, some women wear mildly immodest evening gowns, and there's a scene when a recently showered woman wears only a towel.

MESSAGES TO DISCUSS: "I am satisfied that happiness in marriage is not so much a matter of romance as it is an anxious concern for the comfort and well-being of one's companion" ("Excerpts from Recent

Addresses of President Gordon B. Hinckley," *Ensign*, Apr. 1996). Successful relationships take effort and continued courtship. Though divorce is sometimes acceptable, often the Lord would have us work through marital difficulties (Mark 10:2–9).

END OF THE SPEAR (PG-13, 2005)

This handsomely made, well-acted drama portrays the true story of a group of Christian missionaries murdered by natives in the jungles of Ecuador. It depicts the end of centuries of tribal warfare as killers are converted to Christ through the forgiveness and service of the missionaries' families. In addition to being a powerful, real-world reminder of the power of Christ and His doctrine, the film is also a wonderful exploration of intercultural relations and friendships. The cinematography is lush, the music is phenomenal, and the story is incredible. A 2002 documentary about these events, *Beyond the Gates of Splendor*, is also available.

GRADE: A-

CONTENT OVERVIEW: Some natives are shown nearly nude in loin-cloths (breasts and genitals are covered, but buttocks are seen), though the context is hardly sexual or inappropriate. There's no profanity. There are several deaths by spearing, with some blood.

MESSAGES TO DISCUSS: Healing can come from loving our enemies and doing good to them that have wronged us (Matthew 5:43–44). We are commanded to forgive one another (Doctrine and Covenants 64:10–11). Even the most vicious of people can be changed through faith in Jesus Christ (Alma 24:16–19). One gift of the Spirit is the ability to behold angels and ministering spirits (Moroni 10:14).

ENSIGN TO THE NATIONS (NR, 1997)

This excellent Church-produced documentary chronicles roughly one hundred and fifty years of Latter-day Saint history in rousing fashion. With great production values (the cinematography is rich and vibrant), this hour-long film is full of amazing true stories and faith-promoting interviews.

GRADE: A-

CONTENT OVERVIEW: Nothing offensive here.

MESSAGES TO DISCUSS: The Lord will gather Israel in the Latter-days, the restored gospel being an ensign for them to flock to (Isaiah 5:26).

ERRAND OF ANGELS (PG, 2008)

Gorgeous cinematography of the Austrian countryside, charming performances, and a simple, well-told story highlight this tale of sister missionaries in Austria. The story line delivers a sweet, practical message. Directed by Christian Vuissa (*One Good Man*).

GRADE: B+

CONTENT OVERVIEW: There's nothing offensive here.

MESSAGES TO DISCUSS: "Who am I to judge another when I walk imperfectly? In the quiet heart is hidden sorrow that the eye can't see" ("Lord, I Would Follow Thee," *Hymns*, no. 220).

E.T. THE EXTRA-TERRESTRIAL (PG, 1982)

This classic Spielberg film finds a crash-landed alien befriending a young boy and his siblings, who help the lovable extraterrestrial to evade government researchers and find his way home. A sweeping musical score by John Williams, impressive practical effects, and adorable child performances (including the young Drew Barrymore) highlight this classic sci-fi tearjerker.

GRADE: A+

CONTENT OVERVIEW: As in the case of other 80s "family" movies, there's some moderate profanities here. E.T. gets drunk (as does the child Elliot, vicariously) and technically dies as scientists experiment on him (though he comes back to life).

MESSAGES TO DISCUSS: We can carry departed loved ones in our hearts and memories, where they can continue to inspire the best in us (Helaman 5:6–7). The fictional tale of E.T is reminiscent of the true story of the death and Resurrection of Jesus Christ.

FACING THE GIANTS (PG, 2006)

This faith-based football film from Sherwood Pictures (the Christian studio in Georgia that also made *Fireproof* and *Courageous*) suffers at times from inconsistent screenwriting and acting, but it undeniably invites the Spirit and conveys eternal truths in a powerful way. Alex Kendrick stars as a down-and-out high school football coach whose life, and season, turns around as he devotes his life to Christ and encourages his team to do the same. The football action is well-shot, and the lessons taught are priceless. An excellent film for youth and adults.

GRADE: B

CONTENT OVERVIEW: There is some hard-hitting football action but nothing offensive.

MESSAGES TO DISCUSS: We all have our own Goliaths or challenges that seem insurmountable. However, if we trust in the Lord as David did, we will be victorious (1 Samuel 17:20–51). The Lord blesses us for our righteousness (2 Nephi 1:20).

FATHER OF THE BRIDE (PG, 1991)

Heartwarming and hilarious, this is a tale of an overprotective and miserly father (perfectly played by Steve Martin) who struggles with the fact that his daughter is all grown up, getting married, and having an expensive wedding. Martin Short steals the show as a flamboyant wedding planner. A wonderfully warm little film that exemplifies healthy relationships between parents, children, and spouses.

GRADE: A-

CONTENT OVERVIEW: There are some slapstick pratfalls and a few mild profanities. An engaged couple kiss passionately in front of the bride's father, and a groom rests his hand on his fiance's knee. A father, to everyone's chagrin, makes a worried remark about hoping his daughter and fiancé practice safe sex.

MESSAGES TO DISCUSS: It is natural and right for children to leave their parents and build a life with their spouses (Genesis 2:24). The influence of loving parents lasts for a lifetime (Proverbs 22:6).

FATHER OF THE BRIDE PART II (PG, 1995)

In this worthy sequel, we find middle-aged parents Steve Martin and Diane Keaton pregnant at the same time as their daughter and her husband. The story is a tad far-fetched (of course both women go into labor simultaneously), but it's outrageously funny and quite moving.

GRADE: B+

CONTENT OVERVIEW: There's some mild language. A middle-aged husband and wife start kissing while sitting on the kitchen floor, the scene ends there, but sex is implied (and pregnancy results). An unconscious man unknowingly grabs another man's crotch (played for laughs). A man is taken into a prostrate exam semiconscious; we don't see what happens inside, but he runs out fully awake, fixing his pants while shouting "I beg your pardon!"

MESSAGES TO DISCUSS: Children are among the Lord's greatest blessings (Psalm 127:3–5). He has commanded us to marry and procreate (Genesis 1:28).

FATHERS OF FAITH (NR, 2010)

Covenant Communications presents this new documentary (to accompany its book) and combines some reenactments, truly vintage archival photographs and footage, and interviews with the children of Latter-day Saint fathers who exemplify gospel-centered parenting. Some of the fathers are well-known (Gordon B. Hinckley, Jeffrey R. Holland, David O. McKay), and others less so, but every five-minute story tells of a principle or a virtue that righteous fathers pass on to their children. There are miracles, inspiring stories, and examples of selflessness, kindness, and faith throughout. This is excellent for fathers (and families) of all ages.

GRADE: B+

CONTENT OVERVIEW: There is nothing offensive here.

MESSAGES TO DISCUSS: Fathers should lead without hypocrisy and with patience, kindness, gentleness, virtue, knowledge, and charity (Doctrine and Covenants 121:41–46).

FIDDLER ON THE ROOF (G, 1971)

This masterpiece of a musical finds a family of Russian Jews in the early 1900s dealing with social upheaval, persecutions, and challenges to their faith and traditions. Glorious music and dancing, along with a terrific portrayal of an imperfect but loving family, highlight this bittersweet tale. This is a film that should not be missed.

GRADE: A+

CONTENT OVERVIEW: There is no language or sexuality. There is some drinking. Jews are persecuted, with some stabbed bloodlessly and trampled by horses of soldiers (not overly intense).

MESSAGES TO DISCUSS: It is natural and right for children to leave their parents and build a life with their spouses (Genesis 2:24). We can, and should, speak with the Lord as intimately as we would with a friend (Exodus 33:11). We ought not cast out those who stray from the faith (3 Nephi 18:29–32).

FINDING FAITH IN CHRIST (NR, 2003)

This is a terrific thirty-minute overview of the life of Christ, produced by the Church. The Apostle Thomas (Bruce Newbold) shares with friends how he came to have a testimony of Jesus Christ through the things he witnessed and how they (and we) can come to believe in Him also. At times the supporting performances lack emotional credibility, but the leads are strong, the cinematography is gorgeous, and the recreation of events from the Gospels is first rate.

GRADE: B+

CONTENT OVERVIEW: The Lord's scourging and crucifixion are portrayed in a manner suitable for families, although there's no getting around it being hard to watch as Christ is whipped and crucified.

MESSAGES TO DISCUSS: We don't receive a witness until our faith is tried (Ether 12:6). Faith does not come from seeing (Hebrews 11:1) but from hearing and believing the word of the Lord (Romans 10:17). The Apostles saw the resurrected Christ (Luke 24:36–53). For the story of Thomas, please read John 20:24–31.

FIELD OF DREAMS (PG, 1989)

This powerhouse fantasy-drama finds Kevin Costner giving the best performance of his career as an Iowa farmer who follows the promptings of a still, small voice to replace his crops with a baseball field, allowing for communion with departed spirits who congregate there (it's moving, not creepy). This beautifully shot, warmly acted examination of faith and the eternal nature of family may leave you with tears in your eyes.

GRADE: A

CONTENT OVERVIEW: There is one reference to masturbation, several references to drug use, and some moderate profanities. A man threatens another man with physical violence but doesn't go through with it.

MESSAGES TO DISCUSS: We don't receive a witness until our faith is tried (Ether 12:6). Instead of wishing for more privileges, we ought to be content with what the Lord has allotted us (Alma 29:3). We should listen to the promptings of the still, small voice, for that is one way God speaks to us (1 Kings 19:11–13). We must be willing to endure the criticism and ridicule of others to do what is right (1 Nephi 8:26–33).

FINDING NEMO (G, 2003)

This modern under-the-sea classic from Disney-Pixar finds a clown-fish scouring the open ocean with an amnesiac female named Dory to find his lost son, Nemo. He encounters sharks, stingrays, sea turtles, whales, and much more along the way. It is heartfelt and very funny with vivid animation and unforgettable characters.

GRADE: A+

CONTENT OVERVIEW: There are a few very mild crude jokes and scenes of peril.

MESSAGES TO DISCUSS: Fathers must not try to control their children but allow them to make their own choices while receiving support and guidance (Doctrine and Covenants 121: 34–42).

FINDING NEVERLAND (PG, 2004)

Finding Neverland is a poignant and bittersweet tale of author J. M. Barrie and the friendship he shared with a group of children and their widowed mother, which inspired him to write *Peter Pan*. Johnny Depp and Kate Winslet are in fine form here, as is Dustin Hoffman as a theater producer. Young actor Freddie Highmore gives a brilliantly raw performance. It's a tearjerker, for sure, but it's an uplifting and hopeful one.

GRADE: A

CONTENT OVERVIEW: There is some very mild language. A man enquires whether another man is having an improper relationship with children (in tasteful, not crude, terms). The film deals with heavy themes of death and loss.

MESSAGES TO DISCUSS: Though we lose the ones we love, we can take comfort in the memories they gave us and the things we learned from them. There is a time for all things in life, including laughter, fun, and play (Ecclesiastes 3:1–4).

FINDING REFUGE IN EL PASO (NR, 2012)

This is a charming and informative little documentary that sheds light on a fascinating, though often unexplored, chapter in Church history, namely the 1912 exodus from Mexico. Latter-day Saint settlers who'd fled to Mexico years earlier to escape anti-polygamy laws in the United States were originally welcomed by the Mexican government because of their knowledge of successful desert farming. When rebellions and civil warfare broke out in Mexico, however, the Saints found themselves caught in the middle and fled for their lives to El Paso, Texas, where as refugees they experienced a truly overwhelming display of Christian charity from the citizens of that city. This documentary successfully balances broad historical context with the intimate personal stories of Latter-day Saints tried by poverty and violence, left to the mercy of the Lord and the good people of El Paso. With original photographs, firsthand accounts, perspectives of modern experts, a surprise appearance by a prominent General Authority, and ninety minutes of special features loaded with more information, this is a must-own for Mormon history buffs.

GRADE: B

CONTENT OVERVIEW: There is nothing offensive here.

MESSAGES TO DISCUSS: Charity and brotherly kindness are godly virtues (2 Peter 1:7). The faith gained by trials is precious (1 Peter 1:7).

FIREPROOF (PG, 2008)

Another solid outing from Sherwood Pictures, the Christian production company behind *Facing the Giants* and *Courageous*, *Fireproof* is a wonderful examination of why marriages succeed or fail, and the roles that humility, forgiveness, and faith in Christ play in keeping relationships strong. Kirk Cameron proves a capable lead as a firefighter in a failing marriage who gradually gives himself to God and works to right the wrongs he's done to win back his wife's heart. A few sketchy moments of acting from supporting players notwithstanding, this is an insightful and virtuous film not to be missed.

GRADE: A-

CONTENT OVERVIEW: A husband struggles with pornography (discussed but not seen); he gets rid of his computer to beat the habit. A woman is tempted to be unfaithful while flirting with a successful doctor.

MESSAGES TO DISCUSS:
"Happiness in family life is most likely to be achieved when founded upon the teachings of the Lord Jesus Christ. Successful marriages and families are established and maintained on principles of faith, prayer, repentance, forgiveness, respect, love, compassion, work, and wholesome recreational activities" ("The Family: A Proclamation to the World," *Ensign*, Nov. 1995, 102).

FOREVER STRONG (PG-13, 2008)

Forever Strong is a solid film by director Ryan Little (*Saints and Soldiers*). Based-on-a-true-story, it captures the essence of the values-based coaching style of legendary rugby coach Larry Gelwix (a Latter-day Saint who coached in Highland, Utah) and tells the story of a down-and-out teen, whose drunk driving has had serious consequences. He finds redemption through the principles of work, charity, and integrity while learning to play rugby for Gelwix. Though the film displays some sports movie clichés, it transcends them through the strength of its characters, writing, acting, and filmmaking.

GRADE: B+

CONTENT OVERVIEW: There are some mild profanities and the presence of raised middle fingers, as well as teen drinking and partying (portrayed as detrimental), a car accident, and rough rugby action.

MESSAGES TO DISCUSS: To meet their full potential, young men (and all people) should be strong and active, but, more important, they should be courageous, true, faithful, and honest in all things (Alma 53:20–22; Alma 27:27).

FOURTH WISE MAN, THE (NR, 1985)

This terrifically moving TV movie stars Martin Sheen and Alan Arkin as the fourth wise man and his servant, respectively, who spend their days searching for the Messiah but are continually delayed when the magi cannot help but serve those in need. Though a made-for-TV budget leads to a few less-than-impressive displays of makeup, Sheen and Arkin, indeed all of the key players, give fantastic performances in this extremely moving portrayal of the heart of Christianity: charity.

GRADE: B+

CONTENT OVERVIEW: There are some shots portraying the effects of leprosy. Christ is whipped and crucified (we hear, but don't see).

MESSAGES TO DISCUSS: The greatest gift we can give the Lord is to serve, love, and lift the needy, the sick, the downtrodden, and the heartbroken (Mosiah 2:17; Matthew 25:34–40).

FRANKENSTEIN (NR, 1931)

This classic adaptation of Mary Shelley's novel has lost none of its potency as a thriller and as a tragic morality tale. Boris Karloff gives an iconic performance, eliciting both fear and heartache from the creation turned monster, damned to endure loneliness forever, who lashes out at the world that rejected him. Masterfully directed and impeccably designed, this film is perfect for Halloween.

GRADE: A

CONTENT OVERVIEW: Dr. Frankenstein shouts, "Now I know what it feels like to be God!" though his blasphemy and arrogance proves to be his undoing. The monster is beaten with chains and whips. The monster accidentally drowns a little girl. A man is hanged and another is strangled.

MESSAGES TO DISCUSS: Those who seek to place themselves above God will be cast down, humbled, and brought low (Isaiah 14:12–16). There is good in others that we fail to see if we convince ourselves only of the negative (Mosiah 9:1–2).

FRANKENWEENIE (PG, 2012)

A triumph of animation, character design, and retro filmmaking style, *Frankenweenie* gives us a Tim Burton film reminiscent of the director's deliciously weird early efforts, with plenty of nods to black-and-white monster films. Essentially a heartwarming, boy-and-his-dog version of the Frankenstein legend, the central story is entertaining enough (if about ten minutes too long in the middle), but it's the wonderfully bizarre supporting characters that disturb (in a good way) and amuse the most. The final half hour in particular is a delight, though it may frighten very small children (then again, our two-year-old and six-year-old had a ball). While *Frankenweenie* doesn't quite have the emotional heft it aspires to, it has more than many of Burton's films, and it offers plenty of terrifically stylized fun.

GRADE: B+

CONTENT OVERVIEW: This film contains no foul language or sexuality. A young girl holds dried cat feces in her hand (the texture is disturbingly visible). A dead dog is brought back to life; his appearance is stitched up, and body parts fall off randomly (played for humor). Several deceased pets are brought back to life; some of them become monsters that terrify people (including a fairly intense transformation scene).

MESSAGES TO DISCUSS:

> Religion and science have sometimes appeared in conflict. Yet, the conflict can only be apparent, not real, for science seeks truth, and true religion is truth. There can never be conflict between revealed religion and true science. Truth is truth, whether labeled science or religion. All truth is consistent. There is no conflict—only in the interpretation of fact. It is well to remember that when men make new discoveries in their energetic search for truth, these will always be in harmony with all fundamental and eternal truths. Yes, truth is always consistent, whether it is revealed directly from God to man, through his inspired prophets, or comes from the laboratory through diligent searching of his children and through the influence of the Spirit of the Lord upon them. (Ezra Taft Benson, "Your Charge: To Increase in Wisdom and Favor with God and Man," Sept. 1979)

FROSTY THE SNOWMAN (TV-G, 1969)

This classic TV movie is a Christmas staple in many households, as Frosty the snowman is brought to life and cherished by children who try to protect him from a selfish amateur magician. It has some smart humor that'll tickle grown-ups, while kids adore the story, music, and characters.

GRADE: B

CONTENT OVERVIEW: Frosty melts, in a moment that may sadden children, though he's brought back to life.

MESSAGES TO DISCUSS: When we love someone we put his or her

needs first; neglecting the needs of others in pursuit of our own wants is selfish (1 Corinthians 13:4–5).

GANDHI (PG, 1982)

Gandhi is a sweeping biopic that features Ben Kingsley in a masterful performance as Mahatma Gandhi, the man who pioneered twentieth-century nonviolent resistance on a large scale and worked, among other things, to liberate India from Great Britain and to bring peace among Hindus, Muslims, and Christians. It took home Oscars for Best Picture, Best Actor, and Best Director.

GRADE: A+

CONTENT OVERVIEW: There is some mild language and some racial slurs. British military open fire on a peaceful demonstration, killing many (not bloody). A man is clubbed in the face by a policeman. A man is shot three times in the chest, with some blood.

MESSAGES TO DISCUSS: The hand of God is active in many persons of many faiths.

"The great religious leaders of the world such as Mohammed, Confucius, and the Reformers, as well as philosophers including Socrates, Plato, and others, received a portion of God's light. Moral truths were given to them by God to enlighten whole nations and to bring a higher level of understanding to individuals" ("God's Love For all Mankind," *First Presidency Statement,* Feb. 1978).

Nonviolence is a great demonstration of love that can soften the hearts of our enemies (Alma 24). We should leave judgment to God and work on serving one another and improving ourselves (Mosiah 4:16–22; Romans 12:19; Matthew 7:1–5).

GETTYSBURG (PG, 1993)

This epic four-hour film re-creates the pivotal Civil War battle in great detail, conveying the horror and heroism of war without an overreliance on gore. The period details are impressive (clothing, props, etc.) but it's the dynamic performances by the cast (led by Martin Sheen as Robert E. Lee and Jeff Daniels as Colonel Chamberlain) and the rich screenplay, bursting with ideas and emotion, that make the film truly engrossing. It is adapted from the Pulitzer Prize–winning historical novel *The Killer Angels* by Michael Shaara.

GRADE: B+

CONTENT OVERVIEW: Some mild and moderate profanity along with soldiers killed in combat by cannon, gunfire, and stabbings.

MESSAGES TO DISCUSS: Slavery is an offense to God, who condemns it and established the Constitution, in part, to end it (Alma 27:8–9; Doctrine and Covenants 101:79–80). All persons are created equal before the Lord, regardless of skin color, gender, or social status (2 Nephi 26:33).

GOING MY WAY (G, 1944)

Going My Way is a brilliant musical-comedy-drama starring Bing Crosby as a Catholic priest (Father O'Malley) whose unconventional methods and emphasis on the joyous side of religion ruffle the feathers of his superior. Through Christlike service, the men find some common ground and touch the lives of many, including some rough-and-tumble youth in this charming tale with excellent music (including Crosby hits "Swingin' on a Star" and "Too-La-Loo-La-Loo-Ra"). It's a little slowly paced at times, but it is nonetheless inspiring and moving entertainment. Winner of the Academy Awards for Best Picture, Best Actor, Best Director, Best Original Song, and more. It is followed by the equally wonderful sequel *The Bells of St. Mary's*.

GRADE: A-

CONTENT OVERVIEW: One boy slaps another in the face repeatedly. It is implied that a woman is cohabitating with a man out of wedlock, but the situation is handled tactfully as a priest speaks to the couple about the virtues of marriage.

MESSAGES TO DISCUSS: The purpose of our lives and our faith is to experience joy (2 Nephi 2:25). Children need for adults to guide them lovingly, and not turn away a blind eye to bad behavior (Proverbs 22:6). If we love and serve those who oppose us (Matthew 5:44), enemies can become friends.

GOOD NIGHT AND GOOD LUCK (PG, 2005)

This gripping drama is based on the true story of TV journalist Edward R. Murrow and his public battle with Senator Joseph McCarthy over the latter's "witch hunt" to identify communists in our midst, which was destroying the reputations of numerous innocents in the process. David Straithairn gives a towering performance as Murrow, with Robert Downey Jr., George Clooney, Patricia Clarkson, and Jeff Daniels providing solid support. Presented in gorgeous black and white, this is a wonderfully artistic, well-acted, thought-provoking work.

GRADE: A

CONTENT OVERVIEW: Characters smoke throughout the film (historically accurate for the time). There are a few mild profanities. A husband and wife lie in bed together and talk. She is seen in a slip while they prepare for the day. A man's off-screen suicide is discussed.

MESSAGES TO DISCUSS: Those in the media and the government have a responsibility to tell the truth and not smear the good name of others through gossip (Exodus 20:16). All secrets will come to light (Luke 8:17).

GOOFY MOVIE, A (G, 1995)

This delightfully silly Disney film finds the iconic character trying to bond with his teenage son on a disastrous road trip. Laughs aplenty are found in the screenplay, while the inescapably 90s tone provides for some nostalgic fun.

GRADE: B

CONTENT OVERVIEW: Some slapstick violence. A few comic moments find characters in their underwear.

MESSAGES TO DISCUSS: We should always tell the truth (Exodus 20:16), because all secrets come out sooner or later (Luke 8:17). Fathers should show compassion and understanding for what their children are going through (Psalm 103:13). Children should respect and honor their parents (Exodus 20:12).

GORDON B. HINCKLEY: A GIANT AMONG MEN (NR, 2008)

This biographical account of the late prophet's life focuses heavily on his early years (where he's portrayed well by young actors) and his service as a prophet (using actual footage). While it jumps the middle section of his life almost entirely, it is nonetheless a handsome, well-acted series of vignettes displaying experiences that shaped the man who would be God's mouthpiece. It looks gorgeous (with esteemed LDS director/cinematographer T. C. Christensen at the helm, how could it not?) and it invites the Spirit in its honest portrayal of the man, his virtues, and his faith. The portrayal of his marriage to Marjorie Pay is beautiful, and the final section, celebrating President Hinckley's work as a prophet, moved me to tears. At under an hour, it's perfect for a Sunday afternoon viewing with the entire family.

GRADE: A-

CONTENT OVERVIEW: There is nothing offensive here.

MESSAGES TO DISCUSS: We are commanded to love and serve everyone (John 13:34–35). All people are equal before God (2 Nephi 26:33). We should cultivate a love for fine literature (Doctrine and Covenants 88:118). The Lord reveals his will through prophets (Amos 3:7). Mothers are instrumental in helping children develop faith in God (Alma 56:47–48).

HARRY POTTER AND THE SORCERER'S STONE (PG, 2001)

This first Potter adventure finds the lonely orphan introduced to the world of magic and admitted into Hogwarts, a school where he learns the ropes of being a wizard, makes friends, and faces off with his parents' murderer, the evil Lord Voldemort, in weakened form. This first film does a solid job of setting up the universe and introducing the characters. It's fun and imaginative, but the inexperience of the young actors and an overreliance on groan-worthy humor dilutes its impact, as does its slavish devotion to the book. The series gets much better.

GRADE: B-

CONTENT OVERVIEW: There is some mild language and instances of children in peril. A baby's parents are murdered using an evil curse (represented by a blast of green light and bodies falling to the floor). A dark-hooded figure is seen drinking the silvery blood of a unicorn. A villain crumbles into dust. A friendly ghost removes his head (played for laughs).

MESSAGES TO DISCUSS:

It takes courage to stand up to one's enemies, but even more to stand up to one's friends and family (1 Nephi 7:8). We musn't dwell on what cannot be at the expense of living our life to the fullest with the opportunities we do have (Alma 29:1–3).

> You are well aware of the Harry Potter books and movies by J. K. Rowling. One of the reasons the books are so popular, I think, is that they show children victorious in battle against dark forces. They give readers hope that, even in total darkness, there is that spark of light. Despite the powerful evil arrayed against them, they know they can defeat the darkness. But fundamental to the message of the Harry Potter books is the idea that children don't—indeed, can't—fight their battles alone. In fact, the one gift that saves Harry over and over again is the love of his mother, who died protecting him from evil. Without any question one of those best "defenses against the dark arts"—to use a phrase from the Harry Potter books—is close family ties. Parental love, family activity, gentle teaching, and respectful conversation—sweet time together—can help

keep the generations close and build bonds that will never be broken. (Jeffrey R. Holland, "Let There Be Light," May 2006, Guardian of Light Award Dinner)

HARRY POTTER AND THE CHAMBER OF SECRETS (PG, 2002)

Director Chris Columbus's second stab at the Harry Potter series has a similar tone and pace as the first but manages to thrill and fascinate due to more assured direction and excellent source material. Here, Harry, Ron, and Hermione work to discover how to defeat and find a monster that has been stalking the school's children, while the series' recurrent metaphor for racial equality ("pure bloods" versus "half-bloods") is introduced. The kids are starting to grow into their characters, the humor is less forced, the mythology is expanded in ways that pay off later in the series, and Kenneth Branagh's supporting performance as a narcissistic professor is a delight. This represents a step in the right direction in terms of quality.

GRADE: B

CONTENT OVERVIEW: Some students are "petrified," or frozen with the appearance of corpses (though they are still alive). Ominous messages are written on the walls in blood. There are creepy moments with children imperiled by giant snakes and spiders.

MESSAGES TO DISCUSS: No one is superior to another based on class, race, or gender (2 Nephi 26:33). Our choices determine our quality (1 Nephi 17:35; Alma 13:3–5). True heroes don't need to boast or draw attention to themselves (Matthew 6:1–4).

HARRY POTTER AND THE PRISONER OF AZKABAN (PG, 2004)

The series takes a quantum leap forward in creativity, emotional resonance, and genuine thrills under the direction of Alfonso Cuaron (*A Little Princess*). Here, a convicted murderer escapes and comes after Harry, revealing secrets about his parents' deaths along the way. The lead actors really begin to hit their stride, and though a few moments prove too taxing for their young skills, overall they're terrific. Also stellar are new cast members David Thewlis, Michael Gambon (filling in as Dumbledore for the late Richard Harris), and Gary Oldman. This is the best standalone film in the series, as well as the most visually inventive.

GRADE: A

CONTENT OVERVIEW: Some mild language. Wraith-like "dementors" terrorize children and adults, hovering over them and sucking their souls out of their bodies. There are frightening moments, including a werewolf fighting a dog and a professor seemingly possessed.

MESSAGES TO DISCUSS: Even after death, the ones we love never really leave us (Doctrine and Covenants 130:5). Fear and despair can be dispelled by love, hope, and laughter (1 John 4:18).

HARRY POTTER AND THE GOBLET OF FIRE (PG-13, 2005)

In this fast-paced, action-packed entry, Harry competes in a life-or-death wizarding tournament, the trio begin to take interest in the opposite sex, and Lord Voldemort returns. Though it falls short of the menace and emotion that made the book so gripping, director Mike Newell (*Four Weddings and a Funeral, Prince of Persia*) does a solid job of bringing Voldemort back to life and provides some wonderful action scenes. Where this film really shines, though, is in the portrayal of adolescent hormonal confusion. There is some truly funny stuff here, and Rupert Grint emerges in this film as a very gifted comedic actor. The supporting cast continues to be without equal.

GRADE: B+

CONTENT OVERVIEW: This more-intense installment introduces themes of murder and torture, earning the PG-13 rating, though there's no blood or gore. Voldemort's return is dripping with threatening menace. A teenager's dead body is shown, pale and with open eyes. It's implied that several characters have their first kisses.

MESSAGES TO DISCUSS: Our differences with others are far less important than what we have in common, both in making friends and in uniting against common enemies (3 Nephi 2:12). "Dark and difficult times lie ahead, and soon we must all make the choice between what is right and what is easy" (Doctrine and Covenants 136:31).

HARRY POTTER AND THE ORDER OF THE PHOENIX (PG-13, 2007)

With the return of Voldemort, some of the wizarding world prepares while the rest is in a state of denial and corruption. Harry and his friends fight the system and grow up fast, training for life-or-death battles to protect their world from encroaching evil. By streamlining the bloated novel into a fast-paced political thriller, director David Yates and one-time Potter screenwriter Michael Goldenberg give the story a much-needed urgency, all while brilliantly expanding the fictional world and coaxing the best performances yet from the adolescent stars. Daniel Radcliffe blossoms into a fully-formed and versatile actor. Imelda Stanton's portrayal of Dolores Umbridge is brilliantly two-faced. The climatic showdown stands as one of the most stunning action sequences in the series.

GRADE: A+

CONTENT OVERVIEW: A supporting character is hit with a killing curse and dies. There is an intense snake attack, though it's quickly edited so we don't see much blood. A villain uses a torture curse on a hero. A woman slaps a teen in the face. A teenage boy has his first kiss with a teenage girl, and his friends tease him about it.

MESSAGES TO DISCUSS: Our adversary seeks to isolate us, because when we're alone we don't pose as much of a threat to him. Though he tries to instill fear and misery, the adversary will never know friendship or love and is actually a pitiable figure (2 Nephi 2:27). Unlike him, we have a cause worth fighting for. He may try to fill our minds with evil, but we can cast out his influence by focusing on the things and people that matter most (Jacob 3:2). We all have darkness and light inside of us, but what matters is what we choose to act on; that's who we really are.

HARRY POTTER AND THE HALF-BLOOD PRINCE (PG, 2009)

Harry joins Dumbledore in a quest to discover details about Voldemort's past that could lead to his undoing in the future, all while the teenage trio deal with humorous and heartbreaking relationship woes.

This sixth film deftly balances mystery, comedy, and romance for its first two hours, wisely slowing the pace to give its characters room to breathe and grow before thrusting them into the breathless, chilling, and genuinely heartbreaking last half hour. Michael Gambon here gives the definitive portrayal of Dumbledore, and the relatively light-hearted initial tone serves as a brilliant contrast to the earth-shattering encroachment of evil; it truly feels like there's something to lose, and the stakes are set high for the finale.

GRADE: A-

CONTENT OVERVIEW: A central character is hit with a killing curse and dies; friends and colleagues mourn around the body. A central character drinks a potion that torments him mentally and emotionally; another goes into convulsions when he accidentally imbibes poison. Several male and female characters kiss, at times passionately.

MESSAGES TO DISCUSS: Telling the truth, even when it's painful, often paves the way for the triumph of good (Jacob 7:16–23). Unity and light bring hope which can dispel darkness and despair. Women like men who display chivalry and treat them with respect.

HARRY POTTER AND THE DEATHLY HALLOWS: PART 1 (PG-13, 2010)

Harry, Ron, and Hermione go on the run from Voldemort's forces as they fight to make the Dark Lord mortal again so he can be defeated. If the night is darkest just before the dawn, then this film represents that moment. Significantly scarier and more mature than any film that preceded it, *Deathly Hallows: Part 1* is permeated by despair and punctuated by terror but sustained by moments of loyalty, courage, and love between friends. Every single performance is excellent, and though the film glosses over a couple of important plot points and thus may lose audience members on some minor details, the overall objective is clear. The most visually creative Potter film since *Prisoner of Azkaban*.

GRADE: A-

CONTENT OVERVIEW: Hermione is threatened and tortured; we don't see what happens to her, but we hear her screaming as "mudblood" is carved into her arm. Ron suffers a somewhat bloody injury on his arm and chest. A supporting character dies after he's struck in the chest with a knife. An evil, ghostly vision seeks to inspire jealousy by showing two uninvolved characters kissing (it didn't actually happen) with implied, but not shown, nudity.

MESSAGES TO DISCUSS: We must remain steadfast even in moments of greatest opposition (Doctrine and Covenants 58:2–4). Forgiveness keeps friendships alive. We can face even death with peace of mind if we're pure in heart and have loved (and been loved by) others (Proverbs 14:32; Doctrine and Covenants 135:4).

HARRY POTTER AND THE DEATHLY HALLOWS: PART 2 (PG-13, 2011)

This thrilling, terrifying, heartbreaking, hilarious, and uplifting finale does justice to Rowling's source material. Daniel Radcliffe gives his best Potter performance here. Ralph Fiennes gets to flesh out the evil Voldemort, while Alan Rickman was robbed of an Oscar nomination with his superlative turn as Snape. The action and spectacle is on par with what one might expect from a *Lord of the Rings* film, but it's the quieter character moments that stay with you after the credits roll. Composer

Alexandre Desplat creates a daring score that deftly balances nostalgia with bold originality. Most important to Latter-day Saints, this finale brings chills and even a few tears as courage, kindness, and love make their final stand against darkness. Despite this being the most chilling and violent Potter film, the feeling that emerges above all others is one of being uplifted and inspired to be kinder, more courageous, and more appreciative of those around us.

GRADE: A+

CONTENT OVERVIEW: *Harry Potter and the Deathly Hallows: Part 2* is rated PG-13. It is violent and somewhat bloody, with many dying at the wand of its central villain or in a tremendous battle. A man is killed by a vicious snake attack. A teenage girl is briefly shown dead, having been killed by a werewolf. A teenage boy withstands a vicious attack by the main villain in a final showdown. Corpses litter a battlefield, some of them belonging to long-beloved characters. There is one use of moderate profanity, but no sexuality or nudity. It is too intense for young children.

MESSAGES TO DISCUSS: Our relationships with friends and family continue beyond the grave (Doctrine and Covenants 130:2). Love your enemies, and do good to them that hate you (Matthew 5:44). Look beyond the outside appearance of a person to see his or her heart and intentions (1 Samuel 16:7). The greatest love is to be willing to give one's own life for one's friends (John 15:13). Good people are justified in fighting wars to protect their freedom, their loved ones, and their beliefs from tyranny (Alma 43:45–47).

HENRY POOLE IS HERE (PG, 2008)

Luke Wilson stars in this sweet and simple tale of a depressed and lonely man nursed back to emotional health by the kindness of others and, perhaps, divine intervention. Though the film itself takes an agnostic tone, it allows room for the possibility of God's existence and love and portrays believers in a positive, if eccentric, light. It has a delightful and chaste romance, and even if the plot takes a few contrived turns, the performances and values ring true.

GRADE: B

CONTENT OVERVIEW: There are a few mild to moderate profanities and mild immodesty (woman in tank top and shorts).

MESSAGES TO DISCUSS: Belief in God can comfort us following the death of a loved one (Isaiah 25:8). Sometimes things don't happen for any other reason than to allow us to make a choice.

HERCULES (G, 1997)

This underrated Disney animated film sanitizes the more scandalous aspects of Greek mythology, delivering a family-friendly take on the classic hero as he seizes his destiny to protect the world from gods and titans. It's funny and action-packed, with a delicious turn by James Woods as the villainous Hades and hilarious work by Danny DeVito as Hercules's trainer. It's also a nice love story. The decision to use gospel-style music proves to be an inspired choice.

GRADE: B+

CONTENT OVERVIEW: Hercules fights several villains, with plenty of punching. He cuts the head off of a giant snake and it grows a second head; this sequence is repeated. Singing muses show leg in their robes. Witches share an eyeball, handing it back and forth to one another.

MESSAGES TO DISCUSS: Like Hercules, we have been sent to earth by our father, God, on a mission to meet our full potential and use our talents to help others (Abraham 3:22–25). True heroes put the needs of others first (Alma 15:18).

HERE COMES THE BOOM (PG, 2012)

Though it never quite decides whether it wants to be a comedy or an inspirational sports drama, *Here Comes the Boom* is a worthwhile excursion for those looking for inoffensive fun. It also portrays Christianity positively, which is always a nice bonus. Kevin James stars as a high school teacher who takes up mixed martial arts fighting to earn money to save the school's music program. As a drama, it pales in comparison to the superior films it imitates. Nearly every plot point is wholly predictable, as sports film cliches are trotted out one after the other. A school principal comes across as a one-note villain whose inevitable change of heart feels inauthentic and unearned. As a comedy, however, it fares much better. There are quite a few belly laughs here, including one moment that had me chuckling until my sides hurt and tears streamed down my cheeks. There's quite a few great one-liners, as well as some expertly played physical comedy. The supporting characters are mostly solid; retired UFC Heavyweight Champion Bas Rutten is particularly likable in a warm and funny role.

GRADE: B-

CONTENT OVERVIEW: It has plentiful mixed martial arts fighting and a pair of mild obscenities. A woman reveals some cleavage in a tank top, and men fight shirtless.

MESSAGES TO DISCUSS: The story of Jacob wrestling a messenger of the Lord and earning a blessing, as referenced in the film, is found in Genesis 32: 24–30. With hard work, faith, and unity we can restore atrophied things, people, communities, and systems to their former luster and beyond (Words of Mormon 1:16–18).

HISTORY OF THE SAINTS: GATHERING TO THE WEST (NR, 2010)

This fine thirty-five part documentary from Covenant Communications covers in rich detail the story of the Latter-day Saints from the martyrdom of Joseph Smith to the settling of Salt Lake. This series, as hosted by Glen Rawson, is handsomely produced, always informative, frequently inspiring, and at times very moving. Loaded with journal accounts and other firsthand sources, this fascinating documentary finds unexplored crevices in the well-known stories of the first group across the plains and the Mormon Battalion and takes time to illuminate areas not often studied, such as life in Nauvoo post-Martyrdom and the exodus of later groups. Brought to life with paintings, old photographs, on-location filming, and Rawson's skillful narration, this is a must-have for the Church history buff in your family.

GRADE: A-

CONTENT OVERVIEW: There is nothing offensive here.

MESSAGES TO DISCUSS: The mercies of the Lord are over the faithful (1 Nephi 1:20).

HOBBIT, THE: AN UNEXPECTED JOURNEY (PG-13, 2012)

At the urging of the grizzled wizard Gandalf, eccentric hobbit Bilbo Baggins leaves his comfortable home to join a dozen dwarves in a quest to reclaim their homeland from a vicious dragon in this *Lord of the Rings* prequel, based on the novel by J. R. R Tolkien. In this first of a planned Hobbit trilogy, the simpler nature of the story makes it not as engrossing as the *Lord of the Rings* films, but, taken on its own terms, *The Hobbit* is a terrific fantasy-adventure. It boasts stunning visual effects, wonderful music, intense action, and top-notch performances by Martin Freeman as Bilbo Baggins, Ian McKellen as Gandalf, Richard Armitage as dwarf prince Thorin, and Andy Serkis who continues to delight as Gollum. The film has some pacing issues; it's overlong and drags in the middle as director Peter Jackson expands the story, but it ends on a strong note. Despite its flaws, *The Hobbit: An Unexpected Journey* is an inspiring and uplifting work of pop art.

GRADE: B+

CONTENT OVERVIEW: This film has no sexuality or language. There's one mildly crude joke and some gross-out humor involving troll mucus. As with the *Lord of the Rings* films, there's plentiful battle violence, with frightful goblins, trolls, and orcs stabbed, shot with arrows, and having their heads and arms chopped off.

MESSAGES TO DISCUSS: One of the greatest things we can aspire to is a place we and our posterity can call home (Doctrine and Covenants 38:20). It sometimes takes amazing courage to show mercy and compassion to others (Matthew 5:44; Mosiah 9:1–2; Alma 44:6). It is the small acts of kindness and goodness that keep evil at bay (Alma 37:6; Doctrine and Covenants 64:33).

HOOK (PG, 1991)

Steven Spielberg's moving and hilarious fantasy-adventure finds Robin Williams as an overweight, uptight, and grown up Peter Pan who's forgotten who he is until Captain Hook (a brilliantly unhinged Dustin Hoffman) kidnaps his children and takes them to Neverland. Impressive visual effects, a wondrous musical score by John Williams, and great performances by Willams, Hoffman, Julia Roberts (as Tinkerbell), and Bob Hoskins (as Smee) are particular highlights.

GRADE: B+

CONTENT OVERVIEW: Tinkerbell kisses Peter, who remembers at that moment that he's happily married and is going to fight for his family. Captain Hook stabs a Lost Boy in the chest during a sword fight. A pirate is placed in a treasure chest with scorpions. Several pirates are shot throughout the film.

MESSAGES TO DISCUSS: Parenthood can bring the deepest happiness (3 John 1:4).

HOTEL TRANSYLVANIA (PG, 2012)

A lightweight but warm-hearted Halloween movie that's fit for the entire family, *Hotel Transylvania* is cleverly designed, enjoyably silly, and not the least bit demanding. Adam Sandler lends his voice as Count Dracula, who has long since given up terrorizing and now runs a hotel for monsters deep within a haunted forest. Taking the perspective that horror icons such as Frankenstein's monster and the Wolf-Man are actually lovable and harmless (but persecuted for being different) Dracula's Hotel Transylvania serves as a sanctuary of sorts to protect his friends and beloved daughter from humans. When a backpacker (Andy Samberg, *Hot Rod*) stumbles into the hotel, the film embarks on an exploration of prejudice and acceptance that's actually quite funny and surprisingly moving. The movie expertly parodies the legends of classic horror monsters (it's impressive just how many of them make an appearance here), and while some of the jokes fall flat, Halloween-loving kids and adults will have a ball.

GRADE: B

CONTENT OVERVIEW: *Hotel Transylvania* is rated PG. It has some potty humor (Frankenstein passes gas, the Wolf-Man's children urinate on furniture) as well as some humorous moments with monsters getting injured (Dracula burns in the sun, Frankenstein belly-flops off the high dive and his body parts float away in opposite directions, zombies light on fire and don't care, etc). A few moments might frighten the smallest of children, but the film's tone is light and nonthreatening.

MESSAGES TO DISCUSS: We should refrain from judging those who are different from us (Matthew 7:1–2). Often the individuals and groups we fear have much in common with us; there is good in them that we'll notice if we stop to look for it (Mosiah 9:1).

> Be friendly. Be understanding. Be tolerant. Be considerate. Be respectful of the opinions and feelings of other people. Recognize their virtues; don't look for their faults. Look for their strengths and virtues, and you will find strength and virtues that will be helpful in your own life. (Gordon B. Hinckley, as quoted in *Go Forward with Faith* by Sheri Dew, Deseret Book, 1996, p. 576)

HOW RARE A POSSESSION: THE BOOK OF MORMON (NR, 1987)

This is one of the best films the Church has ever made. In three separate segments, it powerfully demonstrates the value and importance of the Book of Mormon. The first segment introduces the book by portraying the lonely travels of Moroni as he finishes and buries the record. The second tells the story of Parley P. Pratt and how the book impacted his life when he first read it. The final segment re-creates the true story of Vincenzo Di Francesca, an Italian priest who came across a copy of the Book of Mormon without cover or title page. He knew it was true, but he didn't know its name or how to join the church it came from. Excellent acting and production values bring the stories realistically to life.

GRADE: A-

CONTENT OVERVIEW: There are a few moderately violent glimpses at Nephite-Lamanite battles, but there's nothing offensive here.

MESSAGES TO DISCUSS: The Book of Mormon was written for our day (Mormon 8:34–35). Those who read it, ponder it, and pray with a sincere desire to know if it's true will receive a witness by the Holy Ghost (Moroni 10:3–5).

HOW TO TRAIN YOUR DRAGON (PG, 2010)

As a first-rate family-friendly adventure that combines truly stunning visuals with well-rounded characters, *How to Train Your Dragon* doesn't insult the intelligence of young viewers. A young Viking trains to be a dragon killer but instead befriends one of the dragons and brings understanding to the two species. It is moving and uplifting, thrilling and funny, and uses its fantasy story to explore profound themes of prejudice, searching for personal identity, and longing for acceptance by a parent. If this sounds heavy, don't worry; you'll have a great time, and the action is pretty terrific. Listen for a great turn by Gerard Butler as a Viking father.

GRADE: A

CONTENT OVERVIEW: Some human-dragon battles. A main character loses a leg and has it replaced with a prosthetic. Scenes with a giant dragon attacking may frighten the youngest of children.

MESSAGES TO DISCUSS: Rather than judge based on prejudice, we should consider the intentions, history, and heart in getting to know who someone really is (1 Samuel 16:7).

HOW THE GRINCH STOLE CHRISTMAS (NR, 1966)

Looney Tunes director Chuck Jones brings his considerable talents to this animated adaptation of Dr. Seuss's classic Christmas tale with memorable results. The inimitable Boris Karloff provides the narration for this story of a grouchy, holiday-hating Grinch who tries to ruin Christmas for the residents of Whoville by stealing their presents, only to have a change of heart when he realizes the Christmas spirit is about love, not gifts. This is heartwarming and fun.

GRADE: A

CONTENT OVERVIEW: There is nothing offensive here.

MESSAGES TO DISCUSS: No matter what you've done in the past, it's never too late to change and be a better person (Isaiah 1:18). Joy during Christmas comes through service, love, and friendship, not material things.

HUGO (PG, 2011)

Acclaimed filmmaker Martin Scorsese takes his first shot at family filmmaking with *Hugo*, an enchantingly imaginative, artistically dazzling, and emotionally involving work. The story finds a lonely French orphan living in a Paris train station, whose quest to uncover the mysterious past of a broken-down merchant brings healing to them both. I dare not say more as I don't wish to spoil anything. The production design (sets, wardrobes, props) on this film is exquisite, capturing 1930s Paris in lavish detail. The musical score is lovely and the cinematography is stunning. The film's one flaw is that the first act moves too slowly. As the story picks up, the wonderful ensemble cast is given ample opportunity to work their comedic, romantic, and dramatic magic. *Hugo* represents a celebration of imagination, optimism, and fun and is touching, creative, and funny. It's a dream for cinema lovers and will be very enjoyable for others.

GRADE: A

CONTENT OVERVIEW: *Hugo* has a couple of very mild innuendos. There are a few intense moments, but no violence, sexuality, or foul language.

MESSAGES TO DISCUSS: Love casts out fear (1 John 4:18). "If you are lonely, please know that you can find comfort. If you are discouraged, please know that you can find hope. If you are poor in spirit, please know that you can be strengthened. If you feel you are broken, please know you can be mended" (Jeffrey R. Holland, "Broken Things to Mend," *Ensign*, May 2006). Stealing is wrong and has consequences (Exodus 20:15). Drinking can be addictive and damaging to one's health (Doctrine and Covenants 89:5–7). The Lord has given each of us talents and strengths; happiness comes in applying them (Matthew 25:14–30).

ICE AGE (PG, 2002)

The delightful first film in the Ice Age franchise finds a woolly mammoth (Ray Romano), a sloth (John Leguizamo), and a saber-tooth tiger (Denis Leary) join forces to deliver a lost baby back to his family just as an ice age hits. Infectiously silly.

GRADE: A-

CONTENT OVERVIEW: Some slapstick violence and mild innuendos.

MESSAGES TO DISCUSS: If you do good to them that hate you, you never know when your enemies can become your dearest friends (Matthew 5:43–44; Alma 26:29–31).

ICE AGE 2: THE MELTDOWN (PG, 2006)

This sequel finds the ice age ending and our heroes heading to higher ground to escape flooding, finding more woolly mammoths (and a chance to save the species) along the way. The story is fine, but it's the continuing misadventures of the squirrel-rat ("Scrat") as he chases the ever-elusive acorn that provide the best laughs.

GRADE: B+

CONTENT OVERVIEW: A running theme about mating to propagate a species is handled tastefully. There's three uses of the word "ass" referring to donkeys and plenty of slapstick violence.

MESSAGES TO DISCUSS: The Lord meant for all creatures to join, male and female, to multiply and replenish the earth (Moses 2:20–25).

ICE AGE 3: DAWN OF THE DINOSAURS (PG, 2009)

The Ice Age films have never achieved (or aspired to) the greatness of Pixar or the better films in the Dreamworks canon. That said, they've always had a light and easy charm that adults can enjoy right along with their kids. By now audiences know exactly what they're getting from an Ice Age film, and the best compliment one can pay this third film is that it maintains the quality of previous entries. What it lacks in originality it more than makes up for in improved visuals (a pterodactyl chase in particular is stunning), a fun turn by Simon Pegg as a wilderness warrior, and the simple fact that after three films they still keep coming up with innovative mini-stories about Scrat and that acorn.

GRADE: B

CONTENT OVERVIEW: There is some slapstick violence, and mild innuendo, but no sexuality or language.

MESSAGES TO DISCUSS: The greatest love is to be willing to die for someone else (John 15:13). Parents are to take care of their children (Doctrine and Covenants 83:4).

INCREDIBLES, THE (PG, 2004)

While any Disney-Pixar collaboration is worth a look, this one stands out for its surprisingly thorough examination of making a long-term marriage work, the trials and joys of parenting, and action sequences that are more thrilling than those in most big-budget live-adventure films. Though it's dressed as a superhero action comedy, at its core it's a poignant drama about family strife and solidarity. The animation and storytelling are endlessly inventive in this tale of a homebound superhero couple who come out of retirement, bringing their super-powered children with them.

GRADE: A+

CONTENT OVERVIEW: There's a pair of mild profanities. A husband and wife pinch each other's rear ends just off screen. A husband and wife kiss. There is some action violence, including punching, kicking, and explosions, as well as attempted shootings.

MESSAGES TO DISCUSS: Parents should teach their children to not fight amongst themselves but rather to love and serve one another (Mosiah 4:14–15). All secrets will come to light (Luke 8:17). Husbands and wives should love one another (Ecclesiastes 9:9; Titus 2:4).

IRON GIANT, THE (PG, 1999)

An oft-overlooked animated masterpiece by director Brad Bird (*The Incredibles*), *The Iron Giant* is smart, emotional, funny, and nostalgic. The story finds a lonely boy befriending a giant robot from outer space and trying to protect it from the military, who sees it as a threat. It sounds ridiculous, but the characters are so well developed and the story is so well told, I've known plenty of adults who find themselves moved to tears by the end. This is a gem of a film that's well-worth seeking out.

GRADE: A

CONTENT OVERVIEW: There are a few mild profanities, a deer is shot by hunters, a man threatens a small boy, and a giant robot is electrocuted and shot at by tanks.

MESSAGES TO DISCUSS: The greatest love is to be willing to die for others (John 15:13). Our destinies are not fixed nor are they determined by others; we decide what we will become (2 Nephi 2:27).

IT'S A WONDERFUL LIFE (PG, 1946)

This Christmas classic is totally deserving of the praise it receives; those who skip past it while flipping through the channels are denying themselves a profound and life-affirming experience. Troubled businessman George Bailey thinks that all is lost and that he's failed his family and community beyond repair. Considering suicide, he's given a second chance by an angel who shows him what the lives of his family and friends would've been like if he'd never existed. This is a perfect film that has it all: romance, comedy, tragedy, and miracles, with iconic performances by Jimmy Stewart and Donna Reed.

GRADE: A+

CONTENT OVERVIEW: A man slaps a boy in the ears until they bleed. A woman loses her robe and hides naked in the bushes (nothing is shown). A child nearly drowns. A drunken man contemplates suicide by jumping off of a bridge. Several character smoke.

MESSAGES TO DISCUSS: Each of us is placed in this world in the time and place that we might do the most good possible (Esther 4:14). Life is easier to deal with if we share and lighten each other's burdens (Mosiah 18:8–10).

JESUS OF NAZARETH (NR, 1977)

A quintessential film about the life of the Savior, this six-hour miniseries has terrific acting and attention to both historical detail and the biblical text. While Latter-day Saints may disagree with certain elements (the baptism shown is not by immersion, John the Baptist is a bit more wild than we tend to imagine him, etc.), as a whole, there has never been a film that has more thoroughly or impressively told the story of our Savior's life. A reverent tone permeates the film, and Robert Powell makes a believable Christ. It is a treat to experience and contemplate the miracles and teachings of the Lord as portrayed here.

GRADE: A-

CONTENT OVERVIEW: This film is not rated, but the scourging and crucifixion are intense enough to likely warrant a PG-13 rating. Herod's stepdaughter dances for him (then requests the head of John the Baptist) in a mildly sensual scene.

MESSAGES TO DISCUSS: There is no greater love than to be willing to die for another (John 15:13). Following Jesus Christ is the only way to return to Heavenly Father (John 14:6). Christ came to teach the truth, heal the sick, comfort the afflicted, bring to pass the universal resurrection, and make exaltation possible for those who will repent and follow him (Mosiah 3:5–13).

JONAH: A VEGGIETALES MOVIE (G, 2002)

The VeggieTales gang are well-known for their witty and inspiring Christian-themed adventures, and this feature film is no exception. Telling the story of Jonah and the whale, the film is true to the biblical narrative while adding a lot of humorous flourishes and catchy song-and-dance numbers (easier to get away with when your characters are played by cartoon vegetables). The youngest of children to the oldest of adults will have a ball.

GRADE: B+

CONTENT OVERVIEW: There's nothing offensive here.

MESSAGES TO DISCUSS: The Lord reveals his will through prophets (Amos 3:7; Doctrine and Covenants 1:38). Parents may want to use this film as a springboard to study the Book of Jonah in the Old Testament with their children.

JOSEPH: KING OF DREAMS (NR, 2000)

Following their 1998 theatrical release, *Prince of Egypt*, Dreamworks Animation produced this adaptation of the story of Joseph in Egypt, which is far better than its direct-to-DVD status would suggest. Lush animation, good songs, and surprising fidelity to the biblical account make this a worthwhile watch for families.

GRADE: B

CONTENT OVERVIEW: Potiphar's wife tries to seduce Joseph, but the scene is handled tastefully (she says she wants to "be with" him and tries to kiss him, but he resists and flees). Joseph is forcefully thrown into a pit by his brothers.

MESSAGES TO DISCUSS: The story portrayed in this film is found in the Old Testament, Genesis 37–46.

JOSEPH SMITH: THE PROPHET OF THE RESTORATION (NR, 2005)

This hour-long film documents the life of the Prophet Joseph Smith, covering much ground from his boyhood surgery to his martyrdom. Anchored by seminal performances by Nathan Mitchel as Joseph Smith, Katherine Nelson as Emma Smith, Rick Macy as Joseph Smith Sr., and Tavya Patch as Lucy Mack Smith, the film succeeds in capturing the humanity of the man and the mantle of the Prophet. It boasts gorgeous cinematography, excellent music, wonderful period re-creation in sets and wardrobe, and masterful direction by T. C. Christiansen and Gary Cook. There are two versions: the one showed at the Legacy Theater at Temple Square (available on the Doctrine and Covenants Visual Resource DVD through Church distribution) and a slightly different version, available for free online through the Mormon Channel, which provides more details for those not of our faith. Both are excellent.

GRADE: A

CONTENT OVERVIEW: Joseph and Hyrum are gunned down in Carthage Jail in an intense scene that tastefully leaves most to the imagination. Similarly, scenes of persecution (tarring and feathering, jailers talking about rape and abuse) are handled tastefully but without doubt as to what is going on.

MESSAGES TO DISCUSS: Joseph Smith has done more for the salvation of humanity than anyone else except Jesus Christ (Doctrine and Covenants 135:3). We can do all things through Christ, who strengthens us (Philippians 4:13).

JOSEPH SMITH: PLATES OF GOLD (PG, 2011)

By focusing on just a few years of his life, this warm and engaging film gives plenty of details showing just how young Joseph Smith really was when he organized the restored Church of Jesus Christ. It also displays perhaps the most human and rounded screen depiction of Smith yet. The actors fare well, the cinematography is eye-catching, the musical score complements the story nicely, and the script's attention to historical detail is impressive. If the film has a flaw, it's that it often chooses to *tell* instead of *show*, causing it to unfold, at times, like an excellent stage play adapted wholesale and filmed on location. Here's hoping that further installments in director Christian Vuissa's planned trilogy can be more ambitiously cinematic.

GRADE: A-

CONTENT OVERVIEW: *Joseph Smith: Plates of Gold* is rated PG. It has two intense (but not bloody) scenes of childbirth and a moment where a dislocated finger is reset just off screen.

MESSAGES TO DISCUSS: By small and simple things, great things come to pass (Alma 37:6). By the mouth of two or three witnesses shall truth be established (2 Corinthians 13:1). The works of God cannot be frustrated (Doctrine and Covenants 3). Learn wisdom in your youth to keep the commandments of God (Alma 37:35). The Lord gives us no commandments without preparing a way for us to do them (1 Nephi 3:7). We can do all things through Christ, who strengthens us (Philippians 4:13).

JOY TO THE WORLD (NR, 2003)

This terrific short film, produced by the Church, portrays the Nativity story in the Old World and the Americas, as well as the celebration of Christmas in modern times, with music by the Mormon Tabernacle Choir.

GRADE: A

CONTENT OVERVIEW: There is no offensive content.

MESSAGES TO DISCUSS: The Lord came into the world to bring salvation to us all (Isaiah 9:6). He was born unto a virgin (Isaiah 7:14). His birth was foretold by prophets in the Americas as well as the Old World (Helaman 14:2–8). Signs and wonders accompanied His birth (3 Nephi 1:15–21).

JUNGLE BOOK, THE (G, 1967)

Disney's classic animated adaptation of the Rudyard Kipling novel takes loads of artistic liberties with the story, but as a standalone film, it's a swinging good time. Songs like "Bear Necessities" and "I Wanna Be Like You" have been loved for generations for good reason. Indian child Mowgli is raised by wolves and guided through the jungle by Bagheera the panther and Baloo the bear back to the man village, encountering apes, tigers, snakes, buzzards, and elephants along the way. It's loads of fun.

GRADE: A-

CONTENT OVERVIEW: There's some slapstick violence, as well as a potentially frightening scene of a tiger attempting to attack a small boy and scratching ferociously at a bear.

MESSAGES TO DISCUSS:

> If life and its rushed pace and many stresses have made it difficult for you to feel like rejoicing, then perhaps now is a good time to focus on what matters most. . . . Let us simplify our lives a little. Let us make the changes necessary to refocus our lives on the sublime beauty of the simple, humble path of Christian discipleship—the path that leads always toward a life of meaning, gladness, and peace. (Dieter F. Uchtdorf, "Of Things That Matter Most," *Ensign*, Nov. 2010)

KARATE KID, THE (PG, 2010)

This remake is a poignant, moving, and thrilling surprise, with lush cinematography capturing the beauty of China, great action, a solid sense of humor, and wonderful performances by Jaden Smith and Jackie Chan, who here makes good on his stated intention to reinvent himself as a dramatic actor. There's a great deal of thought in the storytelling, morality, and characters. The two-and-a-half-hour running time causes it to drag somewhat, and it stumbles slightly by essentially copying and pasting the ending from the original, but the good far outweighs the bad here.

GRADE: B+

CONTENT OVERVIEW: One of the key messages of the film is that force must be used morally. In order to convey this message, the film contrasts it with violent bullying and the misuse of force. There is child-on-child (and one instance of adult-on-child) violence in this film that serves the purpose of deflating the "fighting is cool" notion some audience members may have. It is gritty and painful to watch, making the film not recommended for very young children who may either be frightened by it or attempt to imitate it. For older children, however, the message of nonviolence should be clear. There are a couple of uses of mild profanity by a child, but these are corrected by his teacher and explained to be disrespectful, so the child doesn't use them anymore. A twelve-year-old boy and girl kiss innocently.

MESSAGES TO DISCUSS: Physical force should be used only in self-defense, never to attack (Alma 43:46) and only with the goal of making peace with one's enemies, not punishing them (Alma 44:1–7). Respect and honor your parents (Exodus 20:12).

118

KID, THE (PG, 2000)

This oft-overlooked Disney film stars Bruce Willis as a self-absorbed image consultant whose life plan is unsettled when he's shadowed by a pudgy eight-year-old version of himself. "The kid" ultimately reminds this self-centered protagonist that he always wanted to fall in love, get married, and raise a family. This one is warm, funny, touching, and well-acted.

GRADE: B+

CONTENT OVERVIEW: Some mild profanity, a reference to hickeys, and a little boy tries to look up a little girl's skirt (we see nothing, played for laughs as an innocent curiosity).

MESSAGES TO DISCUSS: Parents should abstain from being harsh with their children, as it may lead to resentment that lasts for years (Proverbs 15:1). We can only find happiness in following what we know is right (Alma 41:10).

KING KONG (NR, 1933)

The first, and best, version of the giant ape story is a masterpiece of early escapist filmmaking and pioneering visual effects that impress and delight today. An adventure film director takes his actors and crew to Skull Island, where they encounter vicious natives, prehistoric creatures, and a fifty-foot-tall gorilla who they bring back to New York with disastrous results. All these years later, it's still monstrously entertaining.

GRADE: A

CONTENT OVERVIEW: King Kong eats, throws, and steps on many people. He fights and kills several dinosaurs, with some blood. There are a few mild profanities. Kong peels layers off the clothes of an unconscious woman until she's only in a nightgown.

MESSAGES TO DISCUSS: We can find good in anyone if we look for it (Mosiah 9:1).

KUNG FU PANDA (PG, 2008)

Jack Black lends his voice to this hilariously written, gorgeously animated, and surprisingly smart and moving animated adventure about a portly panda in ancient China who dreams of being a martial arts warrior. Dustin Hoffman, Angelina Jolie, Jackie Chan, and others lend their voices to this consistently delightful family film.

GRADE: A

CONTENT OVERVIEW: There is plentiful martial arts fighting, though no one is killed (except the villain, who is humorously disintegrated in the final brawl). There are some mild vulgarities.

MESSAGES TO DISCUSS: We should exert most of our energy dealing with the present, not worrying about the past or future (Matthew 6:34). Do not underestimate your potential, or that of others. When we clear our minds, the truth reveals itself (2 Corinthians 3:14; Alma 19:6).

KUNG FU PANDA 2 (PG, 2011)

A worthy sequel that gives audiences what they want while taking the story and characters in new directions, as Po (Jack Black) battles a new villain while searching for his family heritage. The vocal work is superb. The animation is lush and finely detailed. The action sequences are inventive; there are moments in the battles that are borderline iconic. The music is excellent. Though the film is slightly less laugh-out-loud funny than the original, it packs an emotional wallop that I didn't see coming. Honestly, it is quite touching.

GRADE: A

CONTENT OVERVIEW: This film contains no innuendo or profanity. There is some very mild crude humor and plenty of martial arts kicking and punching. However, the heroes fight only to protect the innocent and are otherwise portrayed as peace-loving. It is implied that a villain kills several characters off screen.

MESSAGES TO DISCUSS: Painful circumstances from the past can shape strong character in the present (Doctrine and Covenants 122:5–7). Inner peace comes from right action and from facing our fears with courage. Adoptive families are capable of love and connection equal to that of biological families (2 Nephi 1:30–32).

LADY AND THE TRAMP (G, 1955)

This animated Disney classic has a high-class domesticated female dog falling for a street-savvy mutt, who takes her on an adventure of discovery. Along the way they help each other grow in surprising ways in this unlikely, albeit charming, romance.

GRADE: A-

CONTENT OVERVIEW: A man is shown smoking a pipe. A dog fights other dogs (seen mostly in shadow). A rat invades a nursery; a dog kills it off screen before it can harm the baby.

MESSAGES TO DISCUSS: We should dismiss no one, for we never know when our influence will lead them to live better lives (3 Nephi 18:32).

LEGACY (NR, 1990)

This hour-long film, produced by the Church and directed by Kieth Merrill, tells the story of the Church from Palmyra in the 1830s to the dedication of the Salt Lake Temple in the 1890s through the eyes of a fictional woman and her family. Though the sheer volume of material to cover in such a short period of time (combined with the dramatic necessity of developing characters, telling their story, etc.) means that very little is explored in great detail, as an overview of Church history it works quite well. Though the screenplay veers occasionally into melodrama, there is a power to the storytelling that is undeniable.

GRADE: B+

CONTENT OVERVIEW: Militia attack Haun's Mill; they surround a cabin and fire into it. We see bodies and mild blood. Children and adults are buried along the trail as pioneers cross the plains.

MESSAGES TO DISCUSS: The Church of Jesus Christ of Latter-day Saints is the Lord's kingdom upon the earth in preparation for the return of the Savior (Doctrine and Covenants 115:4). Joseph Smith was a prophet of the Lord (Doctrine and Covenants 1:17–18).

LES MISERABLES (PG-13, 1998)

Long before it was a hit Broadway musical, *Les Miserables* was a novel by French author Victor Hugo, a work which I believe was divinely inspired and rich in eternal truths. This tale of reformed convict Jean Valjean, the prostitute he befriends, the child he adopts, and the police inspector obsessed with bringing him down has been adapted for the screen numerous times. This 1998 non-musical version is more than worth a watch. Clocking in at just over two hours, Hugo's immense novel is streamlined here, and die-hard fans will no doubt miss some of the omitted peripheral characters. Still, the core of the story remains intact, and the film earns high marks all across the board; the music, cinematography, wardrobes, and production design are superb. Geoffrey Rush excels as Inspector Javert, Claire Danes impresses as Cosette, and Uma Thurman loses herself in the heartbreaking role of Fantine. Liam Neeson is masterful as Jean Valjean. A tender sequence with Valjean nursing the ailing Fantine back to health has to be the most beautifully realized demonstration of Christian charity that I can remember seeing on film. The movie stumbles slightly in the closing minutes; it ends abruptly, rather than with the stirring finale of the book and play, and a character walks away from a situation that he'd never walk away from. Overall, however, this is a moving and well-told story of redemption, revolution, dignity, and compassion amid incredible hardship.

GRADE: A-

CONTENT OVERVIEW: *Les Miserables* contains a few mild profanities, battle violence, a beating, and themes of prostitution that are pertinent to the story and handled tactfully. A sickly woman is seen briefly in her underwear, but the effect is heartbreaking, not arousing. An innkeeper discreetly offers a young girl to a man (sexually), but the man refuses.

MESSAGES TO DISCUSS: Charity is the pure love of Christ; it is displayed in patience, kindness, humility, compassion, and forgiveness, and those who are possessed of it can face death with confidence and peace (1 Corinthians 13:4–8; Moroni 7:45–47). Love leads to a forgiveness of sins (Luke 7:47; 1 Peter 4:8). No matter your past, you can change and be a better person (Isaiah 1:18).

LETTER WRITER, THE (PG, 2011)

A warm and simple tale from director Christian Vuissa (*Joseph Smith-Plates of Gold, Errand of Angels*), this BYUtv production finds a struggling teenage girl rescued by the kind letters of a mysterious stranger, who assures her that she has eternal worth in the eyes of the Lord. With a realistic and moving performance by Aley Underwood (*One Good Man*) and solid turns from the supporting cast, this is a wholesome, touching, and beautifully shot little movie that will inspire viewers to look for more opportunities to be kind in their own lives.

GRADE: B+

CONTENT OVERVIEW: A teenage boy and girl share a kiss. There is nothing offensive here.

MESSAGES TO DISCUSS: The worth of every soul is great in the eyes of God; how great is our joy in bringing souls to him (Doctrine and Covenants 18:10–16).

LIFE IS BEAUTIFUL (PG-13, 1997)

This is an Oscar-winning Italian film about a Jewish father who uses humor and imagination to shield his family from the horrors of the Holocaust. It's a terrific portrayal of loving marriage and parenthood, with fantastic comedic and dramatic acting from Roberto Benigni and real-life wife Nicoletta Braschi. It was nominated for Best Picture, and was the winner for Best Actor and Best Foreign Language Film. Most impressively, the film uses audience knowledge of the Holocaust to fill in the gaps, so no actual on screen violence is shown. This is a wonderfully romantic and uplifting movie. Make sure you watch the original Italian with subtitles; the English voice over is terrible.

GRADE: A+

CONTENT OVERVIEW: A man tells a woman, sweetly and romantically, not crassly, that he'd like to make love with her (they marry and have a son). German soldiers threaten and harass Jewish prisoners. We vaguely see a large pile of corpses, obscured by fog. Persons are shot off screen and prepare to "shower" (actually gas chambers), though their actual deaths occur off screen and there's no nudity. We hear descriptions of Jewish bodies being consumed in ovens.

MESSAGES TO DISCUSS: There are times when lying is morally justified (Alma 43:29–30; 1 Nephi 4:22–23). Humor and playfulness can help us weather the hard times (Ecclesiastes 3:4).

LIFE OF PI (PG, 2012)

Much great art is open to interpretation; it has different meanings for different people. Such is the case with *Life of Pi,* an exploration of faith in God and the nature of belief, albeit one dressed as a fantasy adventure about an young Indian man stranded at sea with a Bengali tiger. While some have found the film to be insulting to religion, I think it displays too much affection for the topic for that to be the case. Rather, I find *Life of Pi* to be an acknowledgment that belief, whatever one's worldview, is a choice one makes to enrich one's life. Director Ang Lee (*Sense and Sensibility, Crouching Tiger Hidden Dragon*) has crafted, along with cinematographer Claudio Miranda and composer Mychael Danna, one of the most artistically stunning and visually arresting films ever made. The story exists in a sort of heightened reality that is accentuated by lush colors and clear images. The performances are excellent and the blend of practical effects and CGI is seamless. *Life of Pi* masterfully balances technical wizardry with an emotionally and intellectually engrossing story. It's thoughtful and challenging.

GRADE: A

CONTENT OVERVIEW: *Life of Pi* is rated PG. It has no language or sexuality. There is a very intense scene of shipwreck, with implications of dozens of persons and animals drowning. There are several startling scenes with animals attacking one another. A man is imperiled by sharks, hyenas, and a tiger. A man describes murder and cannibalism in some detail.

MESSAGES TO DISCUSS: The hand of God is active in many persons of many faiths.

The great religious leaders of the world such as Mohammed, Confucius, and the Reformers, as well as philosophers including Socrates, Plato, and others, received a portion of God's light. Moral truths were given to them by God to enlighten whole nations and to bring a higher level of understanding to individuals. ("God's Love For all Mankind," *First Presidency Statement,* Feb. 1978)

Faith is strengthened when it is tried (Ether 12:6). We choose whether (and what) to believe based on our desires, our personal experiences, and the value of our beliefs in giving meaning to our lives (Alma 32:35–39). We should balance reason and faith (2 Nephi 9:28–29).

LION KING, THE (G, 1994)

Disney's animated masterpiece, loaded with pathos, humor, stunning animation, and unforgettable music, is worth visiting time and time again. Young lion Simba flees after his father's death, returning later to claim the throne from his malicious uncle Scar. The vocal work is superb, and the film is undeniably fun.

GRADE: A+

CONTENT OVERVIEW: King Mufasa is murdered by his brother by being thrown into a stampede. There's a comedic segment involving flatulence and bug-eating. A male and female lion roll down a hill together; he lies on top of her and she licks his face. A villain is killed by hyenas (seen in shadow).

MESSAGES TO DISCUSS: The past can hurt; we can either run from it or learn from it. We are sons and daughters of the king (God) and must never forget who we are (Psalm 82:6).

LITTLE COLONEL, THE (PG, 1935)

My wife was raised on the films of Shirley Temple, and movie buff that I am, I must admit that this was a cinematic blind spot for me. This being my first exposure, I must say that I can see why Temple was such a national treasure. She had spunk and talent to spare. This charming little film has a great deal of humor as well as a surprisingly engaging story: An ex-Confederate colonel refuses to forgive his daughter for marrying a Yankee until, years later, his granddaughter wins him over. Heartwarming, light, and fun, *The Little Colonel* also benefits from a terrific stairway tap dance-off between Temple and African-American entertainer Bo Jangles.

GRADE: B+

CONTENT OVERVIEW: There's nothing offensive here.

MESSAGES TO DISCUSS: Families can be reconciled if we allow forgiveness and understanding into our hearts (Genesis 45:4–5; 1 Nephi 7:20–21).

LORAX, THE (PG, 2012)

Featuring the vocal talents of Danny DeVito, Zac Efron, Taylor Swift, Ed Helms, and Betty White, *The Lorax* is a bubbly and engaging piece of family entertainment. Based on the book by Dr. Seuss, the film follows a young man from a plantless community as he learns the value of nature. The characters and animation are well realized, the jokes hit their marks, the forest creatures are adorably hilarious, and the song-and-dance numbers are absolutely delightful. As an adult viewer, my one qualm with the film is its oversimplification of a complex issue: environmentalism is portrayed as "all good" while entrepreneurship is "all bad." Parents can decide how and if they discuss it with their children, and certainly the notion of appreciating and taking care of the planet is a good one. Plus, there's lots of fun to be had.

GRADE: B+

CONTENT OVERVIEW: The Lorax is rated PG, though it probably should have been G. It has some slapstick violence and mild peril, but nothing else.

MESSAGES TO DISCUSS: The Lord made humans the stewards of the earth; we are to use its resources responsibly (Genesis 1:26–31). The beauties of the earth are God's creation ("How Great Thou Art," *Hymns,* no. 86).

LORD OF THE RINGS, THE: THE FELLOWSHIP OF THE RING (PG-13, 2001)

Peter Jackson's bold and groundbreaking adaptation of Tolkien's trilogy starts here, with young hobbit Frodo Baggins joining with wizards, elves, dwarves, men, and hobbits to destroy the "one ring," which could empower the forces of evil to rule Middle Earth. Brilliantly written, acted, and directed, the film deftly balances an epic scale with marvelously intimate moments.

GRADE: A+

CONTENT OVERVIEW: There is no language or sexuality (there's a chaste kiss between a man and a woman). Some characters drink ale and smoke pipe-weed. There is plenty of battle violence, with creatures and persons shot with arrows, stabbed, and beheaded.

MESSAGES TO DISCUSS: We do not choose the circumstances we are born into, but we do choose what to do with the time that is given to us (2 Nephi 2:21; 2 Nephi 9:21; Mormon 9:28). Even the smallest person can change the course of the future (Doctrine and Covenants 35:13; Psalms 8:2).

LORD OF THE RINGS, THE: THE TWO TOWERS (PG-13, 2002)

The Lord of the Rings trilogy continues as the Fellowship goes their separate ways. Frodo and Sam make an uneasy alliance with the treacherous Gollum (a superb motion-capture performance by Andy Serkis), Merry and Pippin find themselves amid walking, talking trees, and Aragorn, Legolas, and Gimli unite with Rohan to defend the people from Saruman's forces. The Battle of Helm's Deep, as portrayed in this film, is one of the greatest action scenes in cinema history. *Two Towers* is a powerful and engrossing continuation of the series.

GRADE: A+

CONTENT OVERVIEW: There is no language or sexuality (there's a chaste kiss between a man and a woman). Some characters drink ale and smoke pipe-weed. There is plenty of battle violence, with creatures and persons shot with arrows, stabbed, and beheaded.

MESSAGES TO DISCUSS: It is moral and right to fight for one's home, family, and freedom (Alma 48:11–14). There's good in the world, and it's worth fighting for. The power of light (God) overcomes and casts out the power of darkness (the devil) (Mosiah 3:6).

LORD OF THE RINGS, THE: THE RETURN OF THE KING (PG-13, 2003)

Peter Jackson's trilogy comes to a stunning conclusion as the forces of good face off with the forces of evil and Frodo endures the greatest temptation with the help of best friend, Sam. Battle scenes of a scale never before seen highlight this Best Picture winner. The direction is superb, the acting is exemplary, the writing is first rate, the sound design and visual effects are top notch, and Howard Shore's score complements the story perfectly. The film sticks the landing, then goes on needlessly for another half an hour. Still, this overindulgence can't take away from what comes before.

GRADE: A-

CONTENT OVERVIEW: Same as the other films, there's plentiful battle violence (complete with limbs and heads cut off of monsters and warriors stabbed, shot with arrows, and trampled), some chaste kisses, and characters drinking ale and smoking pipe-weed.

MESSAGES TO DISCUSS: We were born with infinite potential; we must seize our destiny and become who we were born to be (2 Nephi 1:21, Romans 8:16–17).

Jonathan Decker

LORD, SAVE US FROM YOUR FOLLOWERS (PG-13, 2008)

The clever title is accompanied by a clever film. Director (and star) Dan Merchant's fair and thoughtful look at America's "culture wars" is Exhibit A for the case that documentaries can be as moving, funny, and entertaining (if not more so) than mainstream films. Merchant, a Christian himself, sets out to examine the damage inflicted to the Savior's cause by those who profess belief but practice hypocrisy and judgment instead of love and service. Equally important, he also investigates how belief in Christ motivates millions to do good and bring healing and hope to others. Interviewing big names from both the right and the left, using archival footage of famous humanitarians and outspoken celebrities, conducting man-on-the-street interviews, organizing a good-natured Family Feud–type contest between believers and secular humanists, and using humorous animation, *Lord Save Us from Your Followers* invites the viewer to be more Christlike and look for the good in those who do not share their beliefs or values.

GRADE: A

CONTENT OVERVIEW: Some bleeped-out profanities, one innuendo, and discussions of mature topics like cruelty toward homosexuals.

MESSAGES TO DISCUSS:

> Be friendly. Be understanding. Be tolerant. Be considerate. Be respectful of the opinions and feelings of other people. Recognize their virtues; don't look for their faults. Look for their strengths and virtues, and you will find strength and virtues that will be helpful in your own life. (Gordon B. Hinckley, as quoted in *Go Forward with Faith* by Sheri Dew, Deseret Book, 1996, p. 576)

The hypocrisy and pride of church members can be a hindrance to the conversion of nonbelievers, while charity and righteousness have the opposite effect (Alma 4:6–14).

LOVE COMES SOFTLY (NR, 2003)

This surprisingly solid Hallmark TV movie finds Katherine Heigl (*27 Dresses*) as a widow who agrees to a marriage of convenience, only to find herself learning to love her husband and his children. This chaste romance is well-acted and well-shot, with positive Christian overtones.

GRADE: B

CONTENT OVERVIEW: A man accidentally walks in on a woman in the bath; we see nothing. There's a brief fistfight. A man falls off a horse and hits his head on a rock; there's no visible blood. A man dies and a woman cries as she mourns him.

MESSAGES TO DISCUSS: The Lord meant for men and women to be together (1 Corinthians 11:11). The Lord will comfort us and bless us if we keep our faith in him (2 Corinthians 1:3–5).

LUTHER (PG-13, 2003)

This has terrific portrayal of the life and mission of Martin Luther, with fine acting by Joseph Fiennes, Peter Ustinov (*Jesus of Nazareth*, Disney's *Robin Hood*), and Alfred Molina (*Spiderman 2*). This film clearly demonstrates the church corruption resulting from the Great Apostasy, as well as the inspired reformation that ultimately paved the way for the Restoration. Luther worked and sacrificed much in his attempts to align the Christianity of the time with that found in the Bible, and the depiction of his faith here is nothing short of inspiring.

GRADE: A-

CONTENT OVERVIEW: One moderate and several mild profanities. A comical drawing shows bare buttocks. Prostitutes solicit priests (not especially crude or graphic) and Luther criticizes the priests for this behavior and the church for tolerating it. Luther marries and is shown in bed speaking with his wife (not a sexual scene). A man is burned alive just off screen, a man burns his own hand in a sermon about the fires of hell, a hanging body is shown.

MESSAGES TO DISCUSS: The original Christian church fell away from the teachings of Jesus (2 Thessalonians 2:2–3; 1 Nephi 13:26–27). Reformers sincerely tried to bring the church back in line with biblical teachings, and God worked in them, but a full restoration of the gospel was needed through Joseph Smith later on (2 Nephi 28:14).

MADAGASCAR (PG, 2005)

Spastic and silly fun, this film follows a group of animals as they escape from a New York City zoo and end up in Madagascar, where they come to terms with their new home and its effect on their friendships. The sequels are actually better, but this first one is good fun.

GRADE: B-

CONTENT OVERVIEW: Some mild profanities, plenty of slapstick violence, and a few mild innuendos (a female hippo comes out of the ocean with sea creatures on her body having formed a bikini).

MESSAGES TO DISCUSS: We can all overcome our natural instincts to make moral choices (Mosiah 3:19).

MADAGASCAR: ESCAPE 2 AFRICA (PG, 2008)

This superior sequel finds our heroes fleeing Madagascar and reuniting with Alex's (Ben Stiller) family in Africa, where another lion threatens his family's claim to lead the pride. Meanwhile, Melman the giraffe (David Schwimmer) struggles to confess his feelings to Gloria the hippo (Jada Pinkett Smith), and Marty the zebra tries to establish his own identity among scores of identical zebras. It's loaded with hilarious non sequiturs and inspired silliness.

GRADE: B

CONTENT OVERVIEW: A large male hippo flirts with a female hippo; the camera focuses on his large buttocks, and he says how he likes large females. There's plenty of slapstick violence.

MESSAGES TO DISCUSS: We all have talents that can contribute to the good of all (1 Corinthians 12).

MADAGASCAR 3: EUROPE'S MOST WANTED (PG, 2012)

This entry conveniently bypasses most of the second film's story, getting our heroes out of Africa and into Europe with the type of economic storytelling that could only happen in an animated film. Once there, this circus-themed sequel successfully unleashes humor (alternating between cleverly witty and randomly bizarre) at a breakneck pace. A tremendous vocal cast and flashy animation (including a brilliantly zany chase scene in Monte Carlo) cover up the lightweight storytelling and the screenplay's disregard for narrative logic. If you enjoyed the other *Madagascar* movies, this one is even better; if you didn't, it's unlikely that the third time will be the charm.

GRADE: B

CONTENT OVERVIEW: *Madagascar 3: Europe's Most Wanted* is filled with lighthearted slapstick violence and peril. There is brief mention of a nude circus and a Russian character exclaims, "That's Bolshevik!" (substituting for "BS").

MESSAGES TO DISCUSS: Sometimes loyalty means sticking together (Ruth 1:16). If we lie to and deceive others, healing and unity can come only through sincere repentance (3 Nephi 30:2).

MANY ADVENTURES OF WINNIE THE POOH, THE (G, 1977)

This quintessential Disney cartoon is witty, silly, and joy-inducing. It recounts many short but connected stories of the classic children's character

Winnie the Pooh, with his friends Tigger, Eeyore, Piglet, Christopher Robin, Rabbit, Owl, Kanga, and Roo. It's simple, nondemanding fun that will appeal especially to younger audiences.

GRADE: A

CONTENT OVERVIEW: There is no offensive content here.

MESSAGES TO DISCUSS: We can find happiness by helping others (2 Philippians 2:16–18); it's better to give than to receive (Acts 20:35).

MARY POPPINS (G, 1964)

Julie Andrews and Dick Van Dyke star in this tale of a magical nanny who brings harmony to a disparate family in this fantasy that's part live-action, part animation, all fun. From unforgettable musical numbers ("Step in Time," "A Spoonful of Sugar," and Van Dyke's classic "penguin dance" scene are among the highlights) to memorable performances, this is one for the ages.

GRADE: A

CONTENT OVERVIEW: There is some cigar-smoking and accidental alcohol consumption.

MESSAGES TO DISCUSS: "No other success in life can compensate for failure in the home" (David O. McKay, Conference Report, Apr. 1935, 116). We can find enjoyment and fun in our work (Doctrine and Covenants 6:31; Ecclesiastes 5:19).

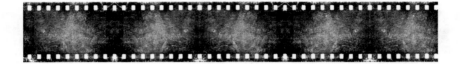

MEET THE ROBINSONS (G, 2007)

This solid, Disney animated film isn't quite as funny or heartwarming as the company's best features, but it's still a worthwhile entry into their canon. A young inventor, left on an orphanage doorstep as an infant, travels to the future in his search for a family to call his own. Wonderful messages about the importance of family, quirky characters, and imaginative adventures make this a treat for kids and adults alike.

GRADE: B

CONTENT OVERVIEW: There are some mildly threatening scenes involving a T. rex, but they're mostly comical in tone. A grandmother shakes her rear end while dancing.

MESSAGES TO DISCUSS: The greatest happiness comes from family relationships. "The family is central to the Creator's plan for the eternal destiny of His children. . . . The family is ordained of God. . . . [It is] the fundamental unit of society" ("The Family: A Proclamation to the World," *Ensign*, Nov. 1995, 102).

MEGAMIND (PG, 2010)

Equal parts witty and delightfully silly, *Megamind* was, for me, a welcome surprise. Turning the super-villain versus superhero genre on its head, it boasts detail-rich animation, dynamically exploiting cinematography that would be impossible with an actual camera, a razor-sharp script that puts an all-star vocal cast to work, and perfect use of classic rock to accentuate the lead character's attitude. *Megamind* provides plenty of fast-paced, laugh-inducing fun.

GRADE: A-

CONTENT OVERVIEW: *Megamind* is rated PG. It contains superhero violence and mayhem, as well as some mild vulgarity. It is, thankfully, free of the crass innuendos snuck into some other recent family films.

MESSAGES TO DISCUSS: There is no happiness in wickedness (Alma 41:10); happiness comes from doing what is right (Mosiah 2:41). There must be opposition in all things; without evil there can be no good and, similarly, where there is evil, good will rise up against it (2 Nephi 2:11).

MIDWAY TO HEAVEN (PG, 2011)

Based on Dean Hughes's novel of the same name, this romantic dramedy finds a middle-aged widower entering the dating-for-marriage scene and resenting the fact that his daughter is doing the same. It's a nice balance of *Father of the Bride*–style comedy, mature romance, and family drama, and the actors are all up to the task. Curt Doussett as the widowed father has charm and very good comedic timing. The movie's greatest strength is his chemistry with the apparition of his deceased wife (played by Melanie Nelson). He still talks with her years after her death, whether as a spiritual manifestation or a mental projection it's unclear. Kirby Heyborne reigns in the comic hamminess that defined some of his earlier roles. On a technical level, the film is solid. John Lyde's editing and Arlen Card's music complement this story well. One of the real treats of the movie, it must be said, is Greg Kiefer's cinematography. I can't remember another film that captured the beauty of central Utah in such an eye-catching manner. The film's only weaknesses lie in pacing and missed opportunities. While there is some overlap between the "daughter dating" and "father moving on with a new love" storylines, the one really only starts after the other is mostly finished, making the film feel like two separate episodes rather than one story. Also, for a film that's clearly taking place among Latter-day Saints, it displays more of the culture and less of the faith. These are minor complaints, however. This is a poignant, funny, and whole-some film that will delight families and individuals looking for something uplifting.

GRADE: B

CONTENT OVERVIEW: There are a few kisses and discussions of mature topics (moving on after the death of a loved one), but nothing offensive.

MESSAGES TO DISCUSS: We are meant to leave our parents and start our own families (Genesis 2:24). It is right for us to seek out companions (Proverbs 18:22).

MIGHTY MACS, THE (G, 2009)

Bogged down by an abundance of sports-movie clichés, occasionally flat dialogue, and uneven direction, the women's basketball drama *The Mighty Macs* nevertheless succeeds as family entertainment thanks to its sincerity and strong acting by its lead players. Telling the true story of a down-on-its-luck Catholic women's college in the 1970s, the film is anchored by the performance of Carla Gugino (*Spy Kids*, *Night at the Museum*), who strikes a nice balance between an independent spirit and a warm disposition as a female coach trying to earn respect for her team and her gender in a sport long considered the domain of men. Some of the characters are underdeveloped, and the plot is predictable; however, there are nice moments of unexpected humor and a refreshing message of interfaith appreciation. The cinematography is lovely and vibrant, and the attention to period detail is sound. What sets the film apart is its positive depiction of faith in God and its female-driven story. *The Mighty Macs* is recommended for fans of inspirational sports movies and religious cinema.

GRADE: B-

CONTENT OVERVIEW: *Mighty Macs* is rated G. It has no foul language, violence, or sexual content. A nun is shown having a beer, and it is acknowledged that a group of nuns used to gamble.

MESSAGES TO DISCUSS: The Lord requires unity if we are to serve Him effectively (Doctrine and Covenants 38:27). Husbands, love your wives, and give of yourselves for them (Ephesians 5:25). We are in the service of God when we are in the service of others (Mosiah 2:17). Our Savior Jesus Christ is a being of joy; we will find happiness if we follow him (3 Nephi 17:20).

MIRACLE (PG, 2004)

This is a gripping true story about the 1980 U.S. Olympic Men's Ice Hockey Team and their historic faceoff with Russia in the height of the Cold War. The film achieves a gritty realism, thanks in no small part to Kurt Russell at his best with his performance as coach Herb Brooks. He plays him as being tough-as-nails with his players and guardedly vulnerable with his wife. *Miracle* also gets a big assist from its script, which refuses to pander to sports clichés and seeks, as much as possible, to tell the story as it really happened while taking time to help audiences know and care about the individual players. The hockey action is hard-hitting and the attention to period detail in the clothing, hairstyles, locations, props, dialogue, and music really takes viewers back to that glorious moment in American history. This exemplary sports film was produced and distributed by Disney with minimal schmaltz.

GRADE: A-

CONTENT OVERVIEW: There's plenty of hockey violence (hard body-checks and a few punches thrown), a few mild innuendos, and plenty of mild profanity.

MESSAGES TO DISCUSS: If we are to reach our full potential and receive glory, we must be willing to endure chastening and punishment (Doctrine and Covenants 136:31). Success comes when all team members work as one, contributing their complementary talents, overcoming petty rivalries, and supporting one another (1 Corinthi-

MISSION, THE (PG, 1986)

This powerful depiction of Spanish Jesuit priests ministering to natives in South America during the 1700s features truly excellent work from Jeremy Irons and Robert De Niro, who are absolutely convincing men of God. Lush cinematography and a stirring musical score highlight this bittersweet tale of the collision between the ways of the Lord and the greed of the world, as Portuguese invaders threaten the peaceful Christian way of life.

GRADE: A-

CONTENT OVERVIEW: While the film is PG, a PG-13 would be more appropriate, with warfare and nonsexual, *National Geographic*-style nudity of indigenous peoples.

MESSAGES TO DISCUSS: Happiness comes from following the way of God, while the way of the world is misery (2 Nephi 1:20; Alma 41:10;

MONSTERS, INC. (G, 2001)

Disney-Pixar presents this original and warmhearted tale that reveals the secret lives of the monsters under the bed and in the closet. Turns out, they're mostly nice and harmless; they only scare children because screams power their city. When Mike (Billy Crystal) and Sully (John Goodman) become unwitting caretakers of a little girl lost in their city, their growing affection for her leads them to rethink their scaring ways. Goodman and Crystal have wonderful buddy chemistry, the mythology is clever, the humor clicks, and the film is ultimately quite moving.

GRADE: B+

CONTENT OVERVIEW: Other than a joke about yellow snow, there's nothing offensive here. Even the "scares" are more funny than scary.

MESSAGES TO DISCUSS: Fear can be overcome by love (1 John 4:18). Laughter and happiness carries great power. "Jesus found special joy and happiness in children and said all of us should be more like them—guileless and pure, quick to laugh" (Jeffrey R. Holland, "This Do in Remembrance of Me," *Ensign*, Nov. 1995, 68–69).

MONSTERS VS. ALIENS (PG, 2009)

Better in concept than in execution, this film is still harmless, non-demanding fun. *Monsters vs. Aliens* is a family-friendly Dreamworks Animation feature that pits classic sci-fi monsters vs. space aliens. It is produced in a 1950s B-movie style showdown with modern humor and the visual flair available through today's computer effects. The story is simple. A meteor crashes on earth, or more specifically, onto bride-to-be Susan Murphy. Some substance from the meteor causes her to grow to fifty feet in height. She is hidden by the government with other monsters (based loosely on the Creature from the Black Lagoon, the Blob, the Fly, and various Godzilla foes), until space aliens arrive, bent on world domination. Outmatched by the alien's technology, the U.S. government calls on the monsters to save humanity from annihilation. All of this is done with a light and fun air, with nothing taken too seriously. Like the best of recent animated features, *Monsters vs. Aliens* is as enjoyable for adults as for children thanks in large part to a constant barrage of jokes (even if there's as many misses as hits) and a stellar voice cast (headlined by Reese Witherspoon, Kiefer Sutherland, Rain Wilson, Will Arnett, Hugh Laurie, Seth Rogen, and, in an inspired bit of casting, Stephen Colbert as the President of the United States). The character design is fantastic, and the film is a visual treat.

GRADE: B

CONTENT OVERVIEW: There is some fighting between monsters and aliens, but the tone is comedic. A woman and a man park in a car; she leans in, trying to kiss him, but he denies her. A woman is hit by a meteor, then grows fifty feet tall, tearing her wedding dress until it's more or less a short skirt.

MESSAGES TO DISCUSS: Women can be as strong and capable as men (1 Nephi 17:2). Sometimes we fear those who are different than us when we really just need to get to know them better to see the good in them (Mosiah 9:1).

MORE PERFECT UNION, A: AMERICA BECOMES A NATION (NR, 1989)

This feature film, produced by the LDS Motion Picture Studio and BYU, chronicles the story of the United States Constitution. With intelligence and clarity, it captures the at-times clashing ideologies, interests, politics, and personalities at play, illustrating just how miraculous it was that the document came to be in the first place. It's well-acted (with a score of recognizable LDS thespians), well-researched, and well-written, with a keen eye for period detail.

GRADE: B+

CONTENT OVERVIEW: There is nothing offensive here.

MESSAGES TO DISCUSS: The U.S. Constitution was inspired by the Lord to establish freedom to make one's own choices and freedom from bondage (Doctrine and Covenants 101:77–80).

MOUNTAIN OF THE LORD, THE (NR, 1993)

This inspiring tale of the construction of the Salt Lake Temple, produced by the Church, is instructive in its history and doctrine as well as a fascinating story in and of itself. Nicely acted portrayals of Brigham Young and Wilford Woodruff are main highlights, as are the solid production values.

GRADE: B+

CONTENT OVERVIEW: A man loses a leg in an off-screen explosion.

MESSAGES TO DISCUSS: The Lord provides a way for us to keep all of his commandments, regardless of the opposition (1 Nephi 3:7). The temple is the house of the Lord; it is a holy place of covenants where only the prepared may enter (1 Kings 9:3; Psalm 24:3–4; Psalm 27:4).

MOUTH OF BABES (NR, 1980)

This hilarious short documentary is sort of an LDS version of *Kids Say the Darndest Things.* Director T. C. Christensen asks primary children doctrinal questions, with adorably funny and sometimes poignant results. A must for family home evenings and Sunday School classes.

GRADE: A

CONTENT OVERVIEW: There's nothing offensive here.

MESSAGES TO DISCUSS: Children can say marvelously wise and uplifting things (Matthew 21:16; 3 Nephi 26:16)

MR. KRUEGER'S CHRISTMAS (NR, 1980)

Legendary Jimmy Stewart's Christmas movie is a touching short film in which an old janitor fantasizes about happier Christmases, singing with the Mormon Tabernacle Choir, and ultimately kneeling before the newborn Savior. Terrific music and a very touching performance by Stewart make this a must-watch during the holidays. Directed by Kieth Merrill (*Legacy, The Testaments, 12 Dogs of Christmas*).

GRADE: A-

CONTENT OVERVIEW: There is nothing offensive here.

MESSAGES TO DISCUSS: We are blessed for visiting the sick, afflicted, elderly, and lonely (Matthew 25:34–40). The Lord was born to Mary to save us from our sins and offer us salvation (Alma 7:10–12; Mosiah 3:5–12).

MULAN (G, 1998)

Mulan is a solid Disney take on the Chinese legend about a girl who sneaks off to take her aging father's place in a war against the Huns, posing as a male to join the army, and saving the nation from destruction. Impressive animation, winning music, a strong and capable female lead, and a humorous turn by Eddie Murphy as dragon sidekick Mushu are particular highlights. Famous Latter-day Saint entertainer Donny Osmond performs the tune "Be a Man."

GRADE: A-

MESSAGES TO DISCUSS: Women can be just as strong and capable as men (1 Nephi 17:2; 2 Nephi 26:33). The greatest love is to be willing to die for someone else (John 15:13). Our ancestors are concerned about our welfare (Malachi 4:6).

MUPPETS, THE (PG, 2011)

Powered by fun music, a slew of celebrity cameos, and a clever script that taps into the essence of the old Muppet charm, this is a delightful return to form for the family entertainment icons originally created by Jim Henson. Costarring Amy Adams (channeling the wholesome earnestness that made her so likable in *Enchanted*), this new tale finds the disbanded Muppets getting together for one last show, mending hurt feelings and old wounds along the way. It's refreshingly optimistic and plenty of fun for both nostalgic adults and children who are getting their first exposure. Though it falls short of the greatest *Muppet* movies, it is easily better than their last few pictures and approaches a return to form for the old gang.

GRADE: B+

CONTENT OVERVIEW: *The Muppets* is rated PG. It is has no offensive language or dirty jokes. There are a couple of moments of slapstick violence (a Muppet is electrocuted, a few punches are thrown in an anger management meeting gone awry; both are played for laughs).

MESSAGES TO DISCUSS: Forgiveness heals relationships (Matthew 6:14–15; 1 Nephi 7:20–21; Genesis 45:3–15). There is strength in unity (Doctrine and Covenants 38:27).

NACHO LIBRE (PG, 2006)

As far as silly, stupid comedies go, this is one of the better ones. BYU alums Jared and Jerusha Hess follow up their hit *Napoleon Dynamite* with this more accessible comedy, starring Jack Black as a Mexican priest who moonlights as a *lucha libre* wrestler. His motives are initially selfish, but he learns to use his passion to help hungry orphans and thus glorify God. Bonus points for pro-Christian elements. Delightfully silly.

GRADE: B+

CONTENT OVERVIEW: There is plenty of comedic *lucha libre* wrestling. A man wears tight pants and comedically flexes his buttocks to impress a woman. A priest sings about breaking his vows of celibacy with a nun (in the context of running away and getting married). There is some flatulence. A man eats egg yolks, a man smears animal feces in another man's eyes, and a man is hit in the eye with an ear of corn.

MESSAGES TO DISCUSS: While violence is, in general, against the will of God, there are times when it is justified and He will come to your aid (Alma 44:2–6).

NAPOLEON DYNAMITE (PG, 2004)

BYU alums Jared and Jerusha Hess write and direct this massive hit about an Idaho loser (fellow BYU alum Jon Heder), his brother, and his high school buddies. The minimalist plot exists to string together a random series of comedic incidents depicting small-town Idaho life. Though it may take multiple viewings to settle into the film's unique rhythm (there's almost no driving force to the plot), those who do will find it oddly endearing and ridiculously funny.

GRADE: B

CONTENT OVERVIEW: A man sells an herbal product said to increase women's breast size. A man thrusts and swivels his hips dancing on stage at a high school election debate. There is some fighting, bullying, and tackling. A man and woman kiss and play "footsie" under the table.

MESSAGES TO DISCUSS: Friends stand by each other and support one another (Proverbs 17:17; Doctrine and Covenants 121:9).

NATIONAL TREASURE (PG, 2004)

Nicholas Cage stars in this Disney-produced, family-friendly hybrid of *The Da Vinci Code* and *Indiana Jones*, as a historian who joins with his best friend and a gorgeous museum curator (Diane Kruger) to steal the Declaration of Independence in order to protect it from a vicious treasure hunter (Sean Bean) and to find the mysterious Knights Templar treasure before him. American myth and American history combine in this action-packed adventure rich with patriotism.

GRADE: B+

CONTENT OVERVIEW: A woman wears a low-cut dress. A man asks if an unmarried woman is pregnant. Villains shoot at heroes but never connect. Decomposed skeletons are seen. A man is shot with a taser. Several characters drink. There are a few mild profanities.

MESSAGES TO DISCUSS: The United States was established as a free land. "That which is wrong under one circumstance, may be, and often is, right under another" (*Teachings of the Prophet Joseph Smith*, sel. Joseph Fielding Smith [1976], 256). Those who have the ability to take action have the responsibility to do so (James 4:17).

NATIONAL TREASURE 2: BOOK OF SECRETS (PG, 2007)

This silly sequel is short on sense (characters change inexplicably and the police are nowhere to be seen in a lengthy car chase and shootout) but it's still plenty of fun as Nicholas Cage joins with his estranged father (Jon Voight) and mother (Helen Mirren) to clear their family name when a Confederate descendant accuses their ancestor of collaborating in the Lincoln assassination. Globe-trotting adventures take them to England, Mount Rushmore, and Washington, DC, and a city of gold. Patriotic fun for the whole family.

GRADE: B-

CONTENT OVERVIEW: It is implied that a man and woman lived together. There is some mild profanity, punching, kicking, threatening, and attempted shootings.

MESSAGES TO DISCUSS: Peace comes from kindness toward and forgiving of others (Ephesians 4:32). We should strive to bring honor to our families.

> In a dream [my deceased grandfather] looked at me earnestly and said: "I would like to know what you have done with my name." Everything I had ever done passed before me as though it were a flying picture on a screen. . . . I smiled and looked at my grandfather and said: "I have never done anything with your name of which you need be ashamed. [George Albert Smith, "Sharing the Gospel with Others," comp. Preston Nibley (Salt Lake City: Deseret Book, 1948), 112; see also "Your Good Name," *Improvement Era*, March 1947, 139]

NATIVITY STORY, THE (PG, 2006)

The Nativity Story is a spiritually edifying film with a keen sense of historical insight, emotional authenticity, and scriptural accuracy. Indeed the only minor change I noted was that the three wise men arrive on the night of Christ's birth, as per tradition, not some time later as recorded in holy writ. Otherwise, the film sticks closely to the Bible. It is also quite moving, as Mary and Joseph go from nervous near-strangers to inseparable husband and wife through persecution, tender service to one another, and the daunting task of raising the Messiah. This is a well-written, well-acted, testimony-building film with gorgeous music and lovely cinematography. I've rarely had such a spiritual experience at the movies.

GRADE: A

CONTENT OVERVIEW: *The Nativity Story* portrays the murder of innocent children by Herod's soldiers, and though the actual violence occurs off screen, the scenes are intense. The scene of childbirth, while not graphic, is also fairly intense. Discussions about chastity before marriage are handled tactfully. Recommended for older children with solid attention spans, teens, and adults.

MESSAGES TO DISCUSS: The story of the nativity as found in Matthew 1:18–25, Matthew 2, Luke 1, and Luke 2. Prophecies of Christ's life and mission (Alma 7:10–12; Mosiah 3:5–15). Jesus will be born of a virgin (Isaiah 7:14), will be the Prince of Peace and, ultimately, the head of government (Isaiah 9:6–7). "I am satisfied that happiness in marriage is not so much a matter of romance as it is an anxious concern for the comfort and well-being of one's companion" ("Excerpts from Recent Addresses of President Gordon B. Hinckley," *Ensign*, Apr. 1996). Husbands are to love their wives and put their needs first (Ephesians 5:25*)*.

> Certainly the shedding of the blood of a beast could be beneficial to no man, except it was done in imitation, or as a type, or explanation of what was to be offered through the gift of God Himself—and this performance done with an eye looking forward in faith on the power of that great Sacrifice for a remission of sins. . . . The ordinance or institution of offering blood in sacrifice was only designed to be performed till Christ was offered up and shed his blood—as said before—that man might look forward in faith to that time. (*Teachings of the Presidents of the Church—Joseph Smith*, Chapter 3: Jesus Christ, the Divine Redeemer of the World, 48–49)

NEW YORK DOLL (PG-13, 2005)

New York Doll is an engaging, sweet, and always entertaining documentary about a punk-rocker-turned-temple-worker whose life of sex, drugs, and rock 'n' roll nearly killed him until he found solace in the LDS Church. Now middle-aged, Arthur "Killer" Kane dreams of reuniting with his band—not for the lifestyle, but for the joy of performance. Along the way, he encounters a lot of old friends whose reactions to his new beliefs are largely positive. This was a Sundance Film Festival favorite and is an inspiring tale that's wholly appropriate for older kids and up. A terrific film for everyone, but may be especially inspiring for teenagers.

GRADE: A-

CONTENT OVERVIEW: *New York Doll* is rated PG-13 for frank (not crass) discussions about the hedonistic lifestyle of rockers (drug abuse and fornication) in the context of this lifestyle leading to misery. Any film that mentions illegal drugs is an automatic PG-13, no matter the context, but this is not an offensive film.

MESSAGES TO DISCUSS: There is no happiness in wickedness (Alma 41:10); happiness comes from striving to develop the virtues God possesses (Romans 8:6; Alma 41:11; 3 Nephi 17:19–20).

NEWSIES (PG, 1992)

This cheesy but much-beloved Disney musical finds a young Christian Bale leading a strike of teenage newsboys against the corrupt Joseph Pulitzer. The singing and dancing are hugely entertaining even if the film's interpretation of history is kind of hokey—but kids won't care; they'll love it.

GRADE: B

CONTENT OVERVIEW: A few minor profanities. Some fighting and black eyes. Teenage boys are seen shirtless briefly. There's a mildly sensual song performed by an older woman.

MESSAGES TO DISCUSS: United in purpose and determined in resolve, people can accomplish amazing things and put a stop to corruption (Words of Mormon 1:13–18).

NIGHTMARE BEFORE CHRISTMAS, THE (PG, 1993)

It's not everyone's cup of (herbal) tea, but this stop-motion animation marvel, produced by Tim Burton, directed by Henry Selick, and distributed by Disney, is annual viewing in many homes for the holidays (Halloween through Christmas). Jack Skellington, the "Pumpkin King" of Halloweentown, wearies of the nonstop gothic scares of his home. Discovering the wonder, joy, and goodwill of Christmas, he hijacks the holiday in a well-meaning but misguided attempt to give Santa a break, with disastrous results. The story is lightweight and the tone may be too dark for some, but there's no arguing the creativity and talent on display, plus Danny Elfman's music is rightly iconic.

GRADE: A-

CONTENT OVERVIEW: Some mild profanity and threatening moments. Some of the Halloweentown residents are scary looking (basically all of the classic Halloween monsters are represented, from witches to werewolves). The film has a macabre sense of humor.

MESSAGES TO DISCUSS: It's never too late to make things right (Ezekiel 33:15–16). When we have grand ideas, we should take inventory of whether we can see it through and what obstacles may get in our way (Luke 14:28–30).

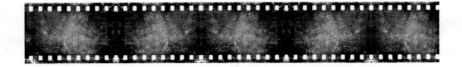

NOBODY KNOWS: THE UNTOLD STORY OF BLACK MORMONS (NR, 2008)

A thoughtful, faithful, and informative treatment on the controversial and misunderstood subject of black Mormons, *Nobody Knows* is long overdue and a most welcome gift for anyone seeking clarification on this matter. With interviews from black Latter-day Saints, both prominent and person-next-door, as well as insights from ministers from other faiths, the film chronicles the history, doctrines, and policies regarding God's children from this bloodline, specifically concerning the priesthood. With testimony and faith, the film clarifies misunderstandings, addresses conflicting statements by Church leaders, and serves as an effective call to repentance for any members with lingering tendencies to look down on those of another race.

The circumstances surrounding the 1978 revelation to extend the priesthood to all races, the formation of the Genesis Group, Jane Manning's incredible example, Brigham Young's support of slavery, and Joseph Smith's opposition to it are all covered here. The film also attempts to capture the experience of being black and Mormon.

GRADE: A-

CONTENT OVERVIEW: Parents should know that there is some mild profanity as well as use of the "n-word" and other racial epitaphs in the context of members telling their stories. I'd also advise parents to watch the film first before showing it to their children, both to prepare themselves for conversation afterward and to determine if their children are mature enough for the subject matter.

MESSAGES TO DISCUSS: All are alike unto God, regardless of race

(2 Nephi 26:33). Righteousness, not skin color, determines one's blessings (1 Nephi 17:35). Racial prejudice is condemned by the Lord (Jacob 3:9; Mosiah 23:7) as is slavery (Alma 27:9), and self-righteousness (Alma 38:14).

OCTOBER BABY (PG-13, 2012)

Conveying several poignant messages with handsome production values and solid acting, the Christian drama *October Baby* tackles the thorny issue of abortion with compassion and intelligence. It tells the story of Hannah, a nineteen-year old who learns that her various health problems are the result of being born after a failed abortion attempt, prompting a quest to discover where she came from. This is a film that handles both lighthearted comedy and heavy drama equally well. Some minor flaws (some underdeveloped peripheral characters, a few too many coincidences in the narrative) don't drag down what is ultimately a powerful story with a redeeming message, namely that every life is precious and that forgiveness and peace are possible through the help and grace of Jesus Christ. This is an uplifting must-see that had the audience I saw it with in tears.

GRADE: A-

CONTENT OVERVIEW: *October Baby* has no offensive content but addresses candidly a mature topic: the heartache that accompanies abortion. A heartbreaking scene finds an ex-nurse describing in detail the pain suffered by an infant fetus. Highly recommended for young teens and up, with strong pro-life and pro-chastity messages, as well as a nice example of interfaith fellowship.

MESSAGES TO DISCUSS:

> This war called abortion is a war on the defenseless and voiceless. It is a war on the unborn. . . . Man-made rules have now legalized what has been forbidden by God from the dawn of time! Human reasoning has twisted and transformed absolute truth into sound-bite slogans that promote a practice that is consummately wrong. . . . People who choose to embark on a journey that leads to parenthood . . . have freedom of choice—to begin or not to begin that course. When conception does occur, the choice has already been made. . . . A woman's choice for her own body does not include the right to deprive her baby of life—and a lifetime of choices that her child would make. (Russell M. Nelson, "Abortion: An Assault on the Defenseless," *Ensign*, Oct. 2008)

The Lord has commanded us not to kill (Exodus 20:13). Forgiving others helps us to feel peace, to be kind, and to be forgiven ourselves through Christ's Atonement (Ephesians 4:32).

ON THE LORD'S ERRAND: THE LIFE OF THOMAS S. MONSON (NR, 2009)

This hour-long biographical documentary, produced by the Church, about the life of President Thomas S. Monson is excellent both as a standalone film and as an unofficial companion to his written biography, *To the Rescue*. *On the Lord's Errand* is uplifting, full of inspiring true stories, and handsomely made, with plenty of footage of and interviews with the man himself.

GRADE: A-

CONTENT OVERVIEW: There is nothing offensive here.

MESSAGES TO DISCUSS: The Lord reveals his will to prophets (Amos

3:7). No matter how many we are called to watch over, we must make time to help, support, and love the individual that is struggling (Luke 15:3–7).

ON THE WAY HOME (NR, 1992)

Okay, it *is* cheesy in parts, but this film carries the power of true principles and some moments of fantastic filmmaking (the scene at the homeless shelter really stands out for me). An investigator family with a tragic past prepares for baptism and reflects on how the gospel of Jesus Christ has restored their hope. This movie displays how the restored gospel can heal family wounds and help them find joy in the present and hope for the eternal future.

GRADE: B

CONTENT OVERVIEW: There is nothing offensive here.

MESSAGES TO DISCUSS: Living by the word of God—His teachings and commandments—leads to the most rewarding life (Matthew 4:4).

ON THE TOWN (NR, 1949)

This superb musical finds Gene Kelly and Frank Sinatra as Navy sailors on leave for a day in New York City, where they see the sights and, along with one of their buddies, romance a few of the single ladies (including *White Christmas*'s Vera Ellan). In the few scenes where it gets serious, it can be a tad melodramatic, but mostly the film is non-stop fun, with rip-roaring song-and-dance numbers and a delightfully silly sense of humor.

GRADE: B+

CONTENT OVERVIEW: A woman incessantly tries to get a sailor to go back to her place; he resists but gives in. Of course, this being a film from the 1940s, once there all they do is kiss. A few scenes show characters smoking. There's some mildly suggestive dancing, but again this being a 1940s film, things don't get out of hand.

MESSAGES TO DISCUSS: The Lord has given us time to battle and work, but also time laugh, dance, and sing (Ecclesiastes 3:1–8).

ONE GOOD MAN (PG, 2009)

Director Christian Vuissa's soul-warming tale of a husband and father attempting to balance work, family, and church responsibilities as a new bishop is short on narrative but long on character study and gentle morality. Much like with his sister missionary movie, *Errand of Angels*, Vuissa offers a deceptively simple story that stirs the heart with realism, genuineness, and virtue. It is ideal for families with teens and older children who have longer attention spans than younger children.

GRADE: A-

CONTENT OVERVIEW: There is nothing offensive here.

MESSAGES TO DISCUSS: The temple is a holy place where only the spiritually prepared may enter (Psalm 24:3–4). Callings come from the

Lord, and He qualifies us for the work if we are humble and obedient. (Doctrine and Covenants 4:5).

ONE NIGHT WITH THE KING (PG, 2006)

As a lavish, gorgeously produced version of the Old Testament story of Esther, this multimillion-dollar production has the feel of the classic Hollywood religious epics. This is both a storybook romance and a powerful tale of faith in God. Tiffany Dupont (Lydia in the first *Work and the Glory* film) does excellent work as Esther, holding her own against acting giants Peter O'Toole (*Lawrence of Arabia*), Omar Shariff (*Dr. Zhivago*), and John Rhys-Davies (*Indiana Jones, The Lord of the Rings*). The sets are enormous, the wardrobe is stunning, the script expands on but is faithful to the biblical text, and the acting is solid. While the film drags a bit in the middle, the powerhouse third act, with Esther putting her life in the Lord's hands as she risks it all to save Israel, hits all the right emotional cords. A faithful treatment of one of history's great women of God.

GRADE: B+

CONTENT OVERVIEW: There is some tasteful discussion of men being made eunuchs. A newly married couple enters their flower-strewn honeymoon suite and kiss (standing up); the scene ends there. A corpse strewn battlefield is seen from a distance (not bloody). Assassination plots are discussed. A man is hit in the face with a cane because he refuses to bow to anyone but God.

MESSAGES TO DISCUSS: This inspiring story of faith and courage can be found in the Book of Esther in the Old Testament. The Lord places us in the time and place where we can do the most good; if we humble ourselves and obey, He will bless and guide us (Esther 4:13–16).

ONLY A STONECUTTER (NR, 2008)

This gorgeously shot short film by director T. C. Christensen (*17 Miracles*) tells the incredible true-life pioneer story of John Rowe Moyle, who worked tirelessly on the Salt Lake Temple even after he lost his leg. Every week he made the commute to Salt Lake, walking over twenty miles to the temple site (and twenty miles back). It's an inspiring tale, warmly acted by LDS film veteran Bruce Newbold.

GRADE: A

CONTENT OVERVIEW: A man loses his leg in an accident; we don't see any gore and the incident is mostly implied, but it is still difficult to think about and there is a little blood (PG-level).

MESSAGES TO DISCUSS: We mustn't let tribulation hinder us in our duty (Doctrine and Covenants 58:2–3).

OTHER SIDE OF HEAVEN, THE (PG, 2001)

This lavishly produced feature film received nationwide theatrical distribution. It tells the story of the missionary experiences of now-emeritus Seventy John H. Groberg (played by Christopher Gorham) as he served in Tonga in the 1950s, facing hurricanes, famine, and temptation, all while exchanging correspondence with his girlfriend, Jean (Anne

Hathaway, *The Princess Diaries*). With a budget of seven million dollars, it's an epic with all the trimmings (including some very impressive special effects). The love for the Tongan people and for the Savior shines out from this film. The scenery and the storytelling are inspiring. It is warmly acted with a good sense of humor and a large heart.

GRADE: A-

CONTENT OVERVIEW: An island girl attempts to seduce a Mormon missionary by disrobing (we see her from the thighs down, no nudity); he quickly looks away and asks her to dress, then proceeds to teach her about the law of chastity and eternal marriage. Some people starve to death and another is taken by infection.

MESSAGES TO DISCUSS: The meaning of life is to come to know Jesus Christ and follow His ways (John 17:3). We must be an example of the believers in word, charity, and purity (1 Timothy 4:12). Sexuality is a sacred and beautiful thing, meant to be experienced within the bonds of matrimony (Genesis 2:24).

OVER THE HEDGE (PG, 2006)

This oft-overlooked Dreamworks Animation film is in many ways an animal version of *The Music Man*, as a charming raccoon deceives a host of woodland creatures whose home was replaced by a suburb while they hibernated. They think he's helping them gather food for the coming winter, but he's actually using them to amass a peace offering of food to save his own skin from a vengeful bear. Of course, his conscience is awakened and their friendship changes his heart. Fun characters, witty dialogue, zany misadventures, and a biting satire of suburbia are particular highlights; with the vocal talents of Bruce Willis, Steve Carell, Wanda Sykes, Gary Shandling, William Shatner, and more.

GRADE: B+

CONTENT OVERVIEW: Slapstick violence, mildly crude humor.

MESSAGES TO DISCUSS: All secrets come to light sooner or later (Luke 8:17). If we steal, we should return what we've taken and apologize (Ezekiel 33:15–16). Families should forgive one another (Genesis 33:3–4).

PASSAGES: TRUE STORIES OF FAITH AND INSPIRATION FROM THE TITANIC (NR, 2012)

This bittersweet and uplifting documentary from Covenant Communications honors the hundredth anniversary of the *Titanic* tragedy by sharing true stories of Latter-day Saints and other Christians who testified of God's hand that night through their faith and actions. Some were spared rather miraculously; others gave their lives heroically to save others or faced death with unyielding faith, finding comfort in the promises of the Savior Jesus Christ. Deftly using dramatized interviews and an impressive array of archival photographs, this roughly thirty-five-minute documentary is perfect for an inspiring and informative viewing on a Sunday afternoon. Equally worthwhile are bonus features, which give fascinating facts about the *Titanic*; *Voices from Titanic* (a mini-documentary in which men and women of faith share, in their own words, their experiences with the ship and their testimonies of the Lord); and *Recollections of Irene Corbett*, a Latter-day Saint nurse from Provo who gave her life to service. In total, there's an hour's worth of material here, enough to justify the purchase price for history buffs and those who treasure inspiring true stories.

GRADE: B+

CONTENT OVERVIEW: Nothing offensive here.

MESSAGES TO DISCUSS: The greatest love is to be willing to die for another (John 15:13). The righteous can face death without fear (Alma 27:28). In certain circumstances, the Lord will intercede to save the lives of the faithful (Alma 57:26).

PETER PAN (G, 1953)

This Disney animated version of the classic J. M. Barrie story has become, for many, the definitive film version of the tale. Colorful characters, memorable songs, and solid pacing make this ideal for repeat viewings. Wendy Darling and her brothers follow Peter Pan and Tinkerbell to Neverland, where they encounter mermaids, Indians, crocodiles, and a band of pirates led by the infamous Captain Hook.

GRADE: A-

CONTENT OVERVIEW: Captain Hook shoots a singing pirate just off screen. Mermaids' breasts are covered by hair and seashell bras. There are sword fights and a crocodile repeatedly attempts to eat Captain Hook. A father loses his temper and shouts at his children.

MESSAGES TO DISCUSS: Thinking positively can help us to deal with, and even escape, our problems (Philippians 4:8). Though we all grow up, we shouldn't lose our childlike sense of wonder, adventure, and innocence (Matthew 18:2–5).

PLAN OF HAPPINESS (NR, 1998)

This Church-produced thirty-minute film, narrated by Henry B. Eyring, explains the origins and usefulness of the Book of Mormon, complete with handsomely made vignettes depicting the stories of Nephi, Enos, Abinadi, Moroni, and the Savior's visit to the Americas. Modern stories and testimonies of those who've read the book supplement the rest. Perfect for family home evening or sharing with curious friends, as it illustrates how the Book of Mormon illuminates God's plan of happiness for our lives.

GRADE: A

CONTENT OVERVIEW: There is some battle violence in depictions of Book of Mormon wars.

MESSAGES TO DISCUSS: The Book of Mormon brings us closer to Christ and helps us to cope with life's trials. Those who study it, ponder it, and sincerely pray about it will receive a witness of its truthfulness by the power of the Holy Ghost (Moroni 10:3–5).

PINOCCHIO (G, 1940)

This Disney adaptation of the classic fable finds lonely carpenter Geppetto making himself a wooden son, Pinocchio, who, according to the promise of a fairy, will become a real boy if he proves himself worthy and follows his conscience, given voice by Jiminy Cricket. Great songs (including the seminal "When You Wish upon a Star") and engaging adventures are par for early Disney, and this is no exception.

GRADE: A-

CONTENT OVERVIEW: There is some drinking and smoking by adults and children, but this is portrayed as being part of a lifestyle that leads to misery. Scenes with a giant whale attempting to eat our heroes and of children turning into donkeys may frighten children. Some cartoon violence. Guns are fired.

MESSAGES TO DISCUSS: Those who speak flattering words and promise self-indulgence without consequence are actually trying to enslave or harm us (2 Nephi 28:21). We meet our true potential when we learn to put others first (Mosiah 2:17). We all have a conscience (a.k.a. the "light of Christ") to help us know right from wrong (Moroni 7:16–17). Honor your parents and listen to their warnings (Exodus 20:12)

PIRATES, THE: BAND OF MISFITS (PG, 2012)

There's a moment in *Peter Pan,* Disney's classic 1953 animated feature, in which Captain Hook shoots a fellow pirate whose singing annoys him. Though the actual death occurs off screen, this moment of dark humor is the kind that pops up occasionally in *The Pirates: Band of Misfits*, the delightfully rowdy offering from Aardman Studios, the animation team that brought us *Wallace & Gromit, Chicken Run, Arthur Christmas*, and *Flushed Away.* That type of dark humor, along with the glamorization of a plundering lifestyle, may be a concern to some parents, while others will find it all to be harmless fun. As for the film's entertainment value, in approaching pirates as if they were the rock stars of the seas, it displays a delightful wit and an infectious silliness. The vocal cast is superb. Most impressive is the stop-motion animation. Taking years to realize, shot one frame at a time, there is a texture to the sets and models that pops out nicely in 3D. The story isn't especially strong, but that matters little when there's so much fun to be had. Well-paced, frequently hilarious, and supported by a toe-tapping rock soundtrack, this *Pirates* film is quite enjoyable.

GRADE: A-

CONTENT OVERVIEW: There is one comical use of the "a-word" as well as some swordplay, punching, and gunfire. A pirate captain is shown drunk. A female pirate with an exposed abdomen swivels her hips seductively while walking, with male pirates ogling her. The only other concern parents may have is that the heroes are thieving pirates thus not very good role models.

MESSAGES TO DISCUSS: We ought not to put the love of riches (Jacob 2:12–13) or the vain seeking of praise (Helaman 7:21) above loyalty to our friends.

POLAR EXPRESS, THE (G, 2004)

Director Robert Zemekis (*Back to the Future*) presents this motion-capture animated version of the classic Christmas children's tale, about a young boy who hitches a ride aboard a train to the North Pole on Christmas Eve. Tom Hanks plays all the adult roles. Though the characters don't quite look as lifelike as hoped for and the film stretches the slim short story into a ninety-minute film with mixed results, there's no denying the film's overwhelming Christmas spirit, the catchiness of its songs, or its appeal to children.

GRADE: B

CONTENT OVERVIEW: There are a few scenes of children in peril.

MESSAGES TO DISCUSS: We won't receive a witness until our belief is put to the test (Ether 12:6). Happiness comes from being grateful for what we have instead of complaining about what we don't (Exodus 20:17; Alma 34:38).

PRAISE TO THE MAN (NR, 2005)

This Living Scriptures DVD release is a thorough and thoughtful overview of the life of Joseph Smith, reuniting the directors of the Temple Square film *Joseph Smith: The Prophet of the Restoration* with most of that film's cast. At about an hour and a half, this well-made and well-acted docudrama, while not as emotionally charged as the Temple Square film, nevertheless is poignant and involving in its own right, and is terrific for gaining (or remembering) the highlights of the prophet's life. Much better than I'd expected, and well worth the purchase.

GRADE: B+

CONTENT OVERVIEW: There is nothing offensive here.

MESSAGES TO DISCUSS: Joseph Smith was called of and inspired by God (Doctrine and Covenants 1:17). He was an Apostle of Jesus Christ (Doctrine and Covenants 20:2), a translator, a revelator, a seer, and a prophet (Doctrine and Covenants 124:125).

PRIDE AND PREJUDICE (PG, 2005)

This gorgeous film adaption of the Jane Austen novel finds Kiera Knightley as a surprisingly good Elizabeth Bennet. The film displays a terrific ensemble, stirring music, lush cinematography, and grand themes about love, marriage, family, and the folly of quick judgment. This one's perfect for date night.

GRADE: A

CONTENT OVERVIEW: A few mild profanities. Some kissing. A few nude figures in Renaissance-style paintings.

MESSAGES TO DISCUSS: Be wary of those who speak flattering words (Proverbs 26:28). People are not always who they appear to be, for good and bad; take the time to get to know them so that you can discern, as the Lord does, the intentions of their hearts (1 Samuel 16:7). Marriage is honorable and ordained of God (Hebrews 13:4; Doctrine and Covenants 49:15).

PRIDE AND PREJUDICE: A LATTER-DAY COMEDY (PG, 2003)

Standing next to *The Best Two Years* as one of the few worthwhile LDS comedies, this contemporary take on the classic Jane Austen novel stays true to the story and characters, even as it transports them to modern-day Provo. I had low expectations when I saw this and was pleasantly surprised at the quality of the acting, romance, and humor. This charming comedy had me chuckling consistently from start to finish. It's apparent that the filmmakers actually understand the pacing and delivery of comedy, and it pays off. It's sweet and silly fun.

GRADE: B+

CONTENT OVERVIEW: There's a mild and comedic fight scene and some kisses. No language or innuendo.

MESSAGES TO DISCUSS: Be wary of those who speak flattering words (Proverbs 26:28). People are not always who they appear to be, for good and bad; take the time to get to know them so that you can discern, as the Lord does, the intentions of their hearts (1 Samuel 16:7). Marriage is honorable and ordained of God (Hebrews 13:4; Doctrine and Covenants 49:15).

PRINCE OF EGYPT, THE (PG, 1998)

While it takes numerous artistic liberties, this Oscar-winning adaption of the Exodus story carries with it a spirit of glory, rejoicing, and reverence that is true in tone to the source material. Don't let the fact that it's animated deter you; this is an ambitious work of art on an epic scale designed to inspire young and old alike. Absolutely stunning visuals and some of the best film music I've ever heard ("When You Believe" won an Academy Award for Best Original Song), in addition to terrific vocal work by Val Kilmer, Sandra Bullock, Jeff Goldblum, Michelle Pfieffer, Danny Glover, Steve Martin, Martin Short, Ralph Fiennes, and Patrick Stewart.

GRADE: A

CONTENT OVERVIEW: A slave is whipped and the aggressor is accidentally pushed off of a ledge (to his off screen death). The massacre of Hebrew children is tactfully handled. Some elements of the story, like the deaths of the firstborn during the Passover and the destruction of the plagues, may be too intense for the youngest of children, but they're handled tastefully.

MESSAGES TO DISCUSS: Parents may want to use this film as a springboard to study the book of Exodus in the Old Testament, where this story is found. Israel was led out of Egypt and blessed according to their faith and obedience, and hindered according to their unbelief and disobedience. Eventually they were led to the land of promise by the Lord (1 Nephi 17:23–35).

PRINCESS AND THE FROG, THE (G, 2009)

Though it's in many ways formulaic (princess character, anthropomorphized animals, happily ever after ending), there's enough here that's fresh and new to make this one of Disney's more interesting recent efforts. For starters, the princess character this time is African-American, and the diversity is welcome. The New Orleans setting allows for the standard musical numbers to be boosted by gospel and jazz styles that are truly catchy and stand unique in Disney's musical canon. The traditional animation, especially the attention to detail in re-creating New Orleans, is stunning, providing some hope for the future of hand-drawn animation in today's computer-generated market. The peripheral characters are amusing. The broad characterization of the prince, however, was less charming to me than it seems meant to be. However, the "princess" is a delightful character.

Fans of classic Disney romances should find much to enjoy here, and others likely won't regret seeing it.

GRADE: B+

CONTENT OVERVIEW: Of concern to parents should be the portrayal of voodoo magic by the villain, specifically with regards to the creepy animation of his "friends on the other side," evil spirits who do his bidding after he makes a pact with them. Drawn as shadows, they are nevertheless quite scary. As an adult viewer, I wasn't especially troubled by it; the voodoo magic is shown as evil and the villain pays the price for meddling with it. Still, this combined with the death of a lovable character (even though he finds happiness after death) the film should have been PG instead of G.

MESSAGES TO DISCUSS: Rewards do not come from laziness, but from hard work (Doctrine and Covenants 42:42). Those who use evil powers via sorcery will die spiritually (Revelations 21:8).

PUSS IN BOOTS (PG, 2011)

If *Puss in Boots* seems like a money-grabbing attempt to capitalize on the successful (if out-of-steam) *Shrek* franchise, it is. But, for an unnecessary spin-off featuring a former supporting character, it's actually pretty good. Though the character, who is essentially an animated version of Banderas's own Zorro portrayal, is not as fresh and funny as he was in his debut in *Shrek 2*, he still maintains sufficient charm and charisma to make for an enjoyable kids' movie that won't have parents checking their watches. He also has a nice chemistry with new characters Kitty Southpaws (voiced by Salma Hayek) and Humpty Dumpty (Zach Galifianakis). As always, the Dreamworks Animation writers have some fun remixing fairy-tale mythology and characters, but in every other respect the film represents a par-for-the-course effort from the studio.

GRADE: B-

CONTENT OVERVIEW: Contains action violence in the form of sword-fighting, hitting, and gun/cannon fire. Like the *Shrek* films it spun off from, there are a handful of fairly adult innuendos meant to go unnoticed by children as well as some mild language.

MESSAGES TO DISCUSS: There is no greater love than to be willing to die for one's friends (John 15:13). Stealing is wrong (Exodus 20:15) and protecting the innocent is heroic (Alma 46:12). A change of heart is possible through true repentance (Mosiah 5:2).

RATATOUILLE (G, 2007)

Disney-Pixar's tale of a rat who becomes a chef in a Paris restaurant is one of their most charming films. Gorgeous animation, smart story-telling, and memorable characters make this whimsical story as enjoyable for children as it is for adults.

GRADE: A

CONTENT OVERVIEW: It is implied that a man had a child out of wedlock without knowing it. Persons and animals repeatedly try to kill a rat (including a granny with a shotgun). A woman slaps a man. A man and a woman kiss.

MESSAGES TO DISCUSS: We mustn't discount the talents and gifts of those who come from poverty or who are different from us (Jacob 2:13–14). All secrets come out eventually (Luke 8:17).

REDEMPTION: FOR ROBBING THE DEAD (PG, 2011)

A hit at the Heartland Film Festival *and* the LDS Film Festival, *Redemption* is a true story of compassion and forgiveness as a sheriff takes pity on a grave robber exiled to an island on the Great Salt Lake in Utah during the 1860s. The cinematography is excellent; notice the gradual "warming" of the colors and tones as the characters approach redemption. Writer/director Thomas Russell has crafted a nicely understated work here; nothing is melodramatic or forced, and the realism pays off nicely. Never preachy or overbearing, some of *Redemption*'s most poignant messages emerge only upon post-viewing reflection. The only real flaw of the film is that some of the dialogue is difficult to hear or understand; however, this is a faith-promoting, virtuous film.

GRADE: A-

CONTENT OVERVIEW: *Redemption* has some bloodless gun violence, some threatening scenes with implications of beatings, brandings, and cutting off part of a man's ears (the scenes end before the actual violence occurs, but the aftermath is shown). A man cauterizes his ear to prevent it from becoming infected. A woman talks about a man making "advances" to her, but the dialogue is handled tastefully and is relevant to the plot.

MESSAGES TO DISCUSS: "Love your enemies, bless them that curse you, do good to them that hate you, and pray for them which despitefully use you, and persecute you" (Matthew 5:44). The body and spirit separate at death but are restored at the Resurrection because of Christ (2 Nephi 9:10–12). Those who show mercy to others will receive mercy from God (Matthew 5:7). "Who am I to judge another when I walk imperfectly? In the quiet heart is hidden sorrow that the eye can't see. I would be my brother's keeper; I would learn the healer's art. To the wounded and the weary, I would show a gentle heart. I would be my brother's keeper—Lord, I would follow thee" ("Lord, I Would Follow Thee," *Hymns*, no. 220).

REMEMBER THE TITANS (PG, 2000)

This outstanding true-story football drama made by Disney stars Denzel Washington as a coach trying to unite black and white athletes in a recently desegregated high school in the 1960s. With warm cinematography, a soundtrack mixing R&B with classic rock, excellent performances all around (watch for a young Ryan Gosling), and hard-hitting gridiron action to go with inspiring messages about unity and race relations, this is a must-see for the entire family.

GRADE: A

CONTENT OVERVIEW: A male athlete kisses a disgusted other male in a comedic scene (he's trying to anger the first; it works). There's some mild language. A player is seriously injured in a car accident. There are some moderate racial slurs.

MESSAGES TO DISCUSS: All are alike unto God, regardless of race (2 Nephi 26:33). Racial prejudice is condemned by the Lord (Jacob 3:9; Mosiah 23:7), as is self-righteousness (Alma 38:14). There is strength in unity (Doctrine and Covenants 38:27; Psalm 133:1).

RESCUERS DOWN UNDER, THE (G, 1990)

Bob Newhart and Eva Gabor return to give vocal work to this superior Disney sequel to *The Rescuers*, which finds mice Bernard and Bianca sent to Australia to rescue a young boy kidnapped by a poacher who's hunting for an eagle. Dynamic and adventurous animation (including some bold "camera" work), witty dialogue, and amusing characters drive the tale.

GRADE: B+

CONTENT OVERVIEW: A child is imperiled and threatened numerous times. There is some slapstick violence.

MESSAGES TO DISCUSS: Heroes come to the rescue of others (Psalm 82:3–4).

RESTORATION, THE (NR, 2003)

This terrific twenty-minute depiction of the First Vision and the Restoration (produced by the Church) is well-acted, well-written, gorgeously shot, and a perfect missionary tool. Stars Dustin Harding (*Joseph Smith: Plates of Gold*) as adolescent Joseph and Nathan Mitchell (*Joseph Smith: The Prophet of the Restoration*) as the adult Prophet.

GRADE: A

CONTENT OVERVIEW: There is nothing offensive here.

MESSAGES TO DISCUSS: By small and simple means great things are brought to pass, including the salvation of many souls (Alma 37:6–7).

If we lack wisdom, we can ask God, who will answer if we ask in faith (James 1:5–6). God the Father and His Son, Jesus Christ, appeared to Joseph Smith to usher in the Restoration of the gospel (Joseph Smith—History 1:3–20).

RIO (PG, 2011)

Boasting eye-catchingly colorful animation, terrific music, and first-rate vocal work, *Rio* provides laughs and enjoyment for adults and children alike. It follows a rare blue macaw, domesticated and raised in Minnesota, as his owner takes him to Rio de Janeiro to mate with the only other of his kind. Once there, they encounter trouble in the form of illegal animal traders and apparent romantic incompatibility. Though utterly predictable (most of these types of films are), the movie is laugh-out-loud funny and has unique characters, impressively realized music and dance numbers, kinetic adventure, enjoyably silly moments, and keen attention to detail in re-creating Brazil's most famous city. In a market oversaturated with computer-animated films, *Rio* is a pleasant surprise.

GRADE: B+

CONTENT OVERVIEW: It has some immodestly dressed women (bikinis) and a man comedically cross-dresses in a "Laker-girl"–style outfit. There is a fight between birds and monkeys that is played for laughs. A villain bird might be intimidating and scary for younger children.

MESSAGES TO DISCUSS: The Lord meant for all creatures to join, male and female, to multiply and replenish the earth (Moses 2:20–25).

RISE OF THE GUARDIANS (PG, 2012)

Engaging, charming, and original, this family-friendly adventure from Dreamworks Animation finds Santa Claus (Alec Baldwin), the Easter Bunny (Hugh Jackman), the Tooth Fairy (Isla Fisher), Sandman, and Jack Frost (Chris Pine) teaming up to protect the world from the Boogeyman (Jude Law), who wants to replace children's hope and happiness with fear. A first-rate family animated film with a creative mythology, solid humor, and tender-hearted morality, *Rise of the Guardians* is highly recommended for children and adults. The animation is gorgeous, the characters are memorable, and the story is surprisingly satisfying.

GRADE: A-

CONTENT OVERVIEW: The Boogeyman turns children's dreams into nightmares (represented by black horses), casts large shadows, and speaks in an ominous voice. The Tooth Fairy punches out one of the villain's teeth. Jack Frost sends the Boogeyman reeling after firing a bolt of light at the darkness he was creating. Santa wields swords but never uses them on anyone. An elf kisses another elf on the cheek (leading the latter to punch the first in the chest).

MESSAGES TO DISCUSS: To understand our purpose in life, we have to know where we came from; in our case, we are God's children and lived in his presence (Job 38:4–7; Jeremiah 1:5), and we were sent to earth to grow and progress through obedience (Abraham 3:22–25). We can get along with people who are different from us if we take the time to get to know them, understand them, and see the good in them (Mosiah 9:1; Helaman 6:7–8). Love and laughter cast out fear (1 John 4:18).

ROBIN HOOD (G, 1973)

Disney's animated take on the legend puts anthropomorphized animals in all of the roles (Robin and Marian are foxes, Little John is a bear, Prince John is a cowardly lion, etc). This is rowdy, charming fun, from the thumb-sucking villain to the terrific folk songs that pop up every few minutes. It will delight kids and adults.

GRADE: A-

CONTENT OVERVIEW: There is some slapstick violence, and arrows are shot in the direction of the heroes. There is one use of mild profanity. The serpent Hiss gets drunk when he's crammed into a barrel of wine.

MESSAGES TO DISCUSS: "That which is wrong under one circumstance may be, and often is, right under another" (Joseph Smith, in *The Personal Writings of Joseph Smith*, Dean C. Jessee [editor], p. 507–9).

ROCKETEER, THE (PG, 1991)

This rip-roaring, live-action Disney adventure is created in the style of Old Hollywood serials. It finds a pilot (Billy Cambell) in the 1930s discovering a rocket pack, designed by Howard Hughes, that enables him to fly. This all-American hero must protect the invention from mobsters and Nazi agents, including one undercover as a Hollywood actor (a wonderfully nasty Timothy Dalton), while fighting to save his girlfriend (Jennifer Connelly). The visual effects hold up, the action sequences thrill (though the film could've used more of them), and James Horner's musical score soars. Alan Arkin gives a fun supporting turn as a mechanic.

GRADE: B+

CONTENT OVERVIEW: Some persons are shot in gunfights. A giant, gruesome henchman kills several people, folding one in half (we only get glimpses of the aftermath) and attacking a wounded man in a hospital bed (we hear screaming but don't see the actual murder). A woman wears a somewhat revealing cocktail dress. There is some mild profanity and one moderate profanity. A few people drink at a night-club. A woman asks a villain to help her unzip her dress, he comes over to do so and she hits him with a vase, knocking him out.

MESSAGES TO DISCUSS: Men and women are meant to be together (1 Corinthians 11:11). Evil must be resisted, even with force (Alma 48:13–14).

ROCKY BALBOA (PG, 2006)

With this poignant finale, writer/director/star Sylvester Stallone redeems the franchise and reminds us of two things: First, before he chose a career of empty action movies, he was once nominated for Best Actor. Second, the reason the first two movies were so great was that they were character-driven, tender love stories about Rocky and Adrian. This is both a worthwhile stand-alone film and an outstanding bookend to the Rocky saga, with poignant messages about aging, mortality, and love that transcends death. Rocky is a devoted father, a good friend, and a loyal husband. This film finds him performing random acts of kindness, displaying good sportsmanship, and cherishing his Christian faith. Though this film isn't so much about boxing as it is about perseverance, it is worth noting that the final fight is both the most realistic since the first film and the most thrilling since the second, as for the first time in years, the audience doesn't know the outcome; our aged hero could win, lose, or even die. Much more than just a Rocky movie, this is an exemplary family drama, period. Don't miss it, whether you're a fan of the series or have never seen any of them.

GRADE: A-

CONTENT OVERVIEW: There are a few mild and moderate profanities and a few characters drink. A boxing scene is fairly intense and brutal, but doesn't go beyond the limits of the PG rating. There are a few glimpses of immodestly dressed "ringside girls."

MESSAGES TO DISCUSS: Glory awaits if we endure well the tough times of life (Doctrine and Covenants 58:2–4). Charity means to help others without expectation of praise or reward (Matthew 6:1–4). Fathers should teach their children about life and the right way to go (Proverbs 22:6).

ROMAN HOLIDAY (NR, 1953)

When it comes to romance, Old Hollywood trumps modern Hollywood, hands down. Audrey Hepburn and Gregory Peck star, respectively, as a princess-in-disguise and the American journalist she falls for while ditching affairs of state in Rome. This is one of my all-time favorite love stories: it's whimsical, bittersweet, charming, and ultimately a tale of utmost integrity.

GRADE: A+

CONTENT OVERVIEW: A sedated princess spends the night in a man's apartment; she sleeps in the bed and he sleeps on the couch (he innocently took her in to spare her from sleeping in the street); they later discuss how her sleeping over might look to others. There is a comical fistfight at a dance and some smoking and drinking.

MESSAGES TO DISCUSS: Coming to love and appreciate others helps us to overcome our own selfishness and put their needs first (Mosiah 9:1).

ROOKIE, THE (G, 2002)

Dennis Quaid stars in this Disney baseball drama about an aging high school coach with a wicked fastball who's given a shot at the pros. Quaid gives a great performance, the teens are great fun, and the film has one of the best portrayals of a supportive marriage I've ever seen.

GRADE: B+

CONTENT OVERVIEW: There are a few mild profanities. A man pinches his wife's rear.

MESSAGES TO DISCUSS: Husbands and wives gain strength from loving and supporting one another (Ephesians 5:33).

RUDOLPH THE RED-NOSED REINDEER (G, 1964)

The Christmas carol gets an expanded story in this stop-motion animated TV movie, rightfully an annual classic in many households. The red nose, the teasing, the snowstorm, and Rudolph leading the sleigh are all here, but so are original elements: a singing snowman, an angry Yeti, the Island of Misfit Toys, and an elf who wants to be a dentist. It's all light and frothy fun that kids will want to revisit and adults may find themselves enjoying. The raw and unpolished animation is just part of the charm.

GRADE: B

CONTENT OVERVIEW: The roaring Abominable Snowman may frighten toddlers and infants.

MESSAGES TO DISCUSS: Though we may sometimes feel like we don't fit in, we're all equal before God (Galatians 3:28) and we all have unique talents to contribute (Doctrine and Covenants 46:11).

SAINTS AND SOLDIERS (PG-13, 2003)

Director Ryan Little makes a one-million-dollar budget look like forty million in this harrowing World War II tale, based on actual events. A Latter-day Saint sharpshooter (Corbin Allred), in a fantastic performance, clashes and bonds with an atheist medic as they and three other soldiers attempt to evade German soldiers and bring classified intelligence to the Allies. The film's message about faith and kindness, even in times of war, strikes a resonant chord. It shows the practical, real-world value of faith in the Savior and His gospel, without being heavy-handed or preachy. High-quality filmmaking, cinematography, music, and acting make this an exemplary example of what "Mormon cinema" can be.

GRADE: A+

CONTENT OVERVIEW: There's some mild profanity and a good deal of (mostly bloodless) war violence. A man experiencing post-traumatic stress has some frightful visions.

MESSAGES TO DISCUSS: If we are a good example of the believers, we may inspire others to take interest in our faith (1 Timothy 4:12). The Lord loves people of all nations, and none is seen as superior in his eyes, though he does favor and bless the righteous (1 Nephi 17:33).

SAINTS AND SOLDIERS: AIRBORNE CREED (PG-13, 2012)

Not a direct sequel to *Saints and Soldiers*, this WWII tale nevertheless shares that film's commitment to examining people's capacity for humanity and compassion amidst the horror and depravity of war. This time, a trio of paratroopers have landed behind enemy lines and must get back, but the plot is really just a vessel for character study. The story seems to meander, but in the last half hour the various story threads come together in an incredibly satisfying way. Heartbreaking, gorgeously shot, and marvelously acted, *Saints and Soldiers: Airborne Creed* is in many ways a subtler work than its predecessor. It's not as action driven (although it features one phenomenal fistfight and a few battles), and its pace is more reflective, but thoughtful audiences will find much to appreciate and be inspired by here.

GRADE: A-

CONTENT OVERVIEW: This film has some war violence, including a brutal fistfight and multiple shootings. There is some mild language.

MESSAGES TO DISCUSS: We serve God best by helping others (Matthew 25:40; Mosiah 2:17). Those who we think deserve our hate, in God's eyes, deserve our mercy, love, and kindness (Mosiah 9:1; Matthew 5:43–46).

SENSE AND SENSIBILITY (PG, 1995)

This entertaining film version of the Jane Austen novel stars Emma Thompson, Kate Winslet, Hugh Grant, and, in a rare romantic lead, Alan Rickman. The performances are great and the film emphasizes the deep, caring, considerate love that transcends romance. It has all of the warmth, wit, and emotion audiences (and readers) have come to expect from an Austen story.

GRADE: A

CONTENT OVERVIEW: There are thematic elements regarding unwed pregnancy (in the context of it causing heartache and difficulty).

MESSAGES TO DISCUSS: True, abiding love is characterized by patience, concern for another's well-being, kindness, humility, virtue, and selflessness (1 Corinthians 13:4–8).

SHADOWLANDS (PG, 1993)

This is an effective tear-jerker about Christian intellectual C. S. Lewis and the love of his life, played to perfection by Anthony Hopkins and Debra Winger, respectively. The film positively portrays Lewis's Christian faith and has terrific messages about love, marriage, loss, and belief. Hopkins is terrific, as always, and Winger will knock your socks off with a performance that earned her a Best Actress nomination. It's wholesome and uplifting.

GRADE: A+

CONTENT OVERVIEW: A few characters smoke and drink. A main character dies from illness and the film explores the emotional fallout. There is a very tasteful scene where a wife explains to her new husband, who's never been with a woman, that she'll be sleeping in his bed now.

MESSAGES TO DISCUSS: When we lose a loved one, we hurt because we loved; pain is the price of loving them, but our sorrow can be swallowed up in Christ's victory over death (Mosiah 16:8; Alma 28:12).

SILENT NIGHT (PG, 2012)

The latest from acclaimed LDS filmmaker Christian Vuissa, *Silent Night* is a story told with passion and subtle patriotism. Vuissa is from Austria, and this is the true story of Austrian priest Joseph Mohr, and how his ministry among the people of a small town drew him closer to Christ and inspired him to write the classic hymn "Silent Night." Though the apparent use of native actors in an English-language film means that some dialogue is occasionally lost in Austrian accents, this is mostly not a problem and well worth it for the authenticity it yields.

It must also be said that the actors, unknown at least in the United States, carry the film effortlessly, conveying wonderful subtlety as the natures of faith, doubt, misery, hope, and charity are brilliantly explored. They are aided by an excellent screenplay, gorgeous cinematography, and, as expected, wonderful music. This is a sublime and inspiring true story, skillfully made and sweetly acted. You'll want to watch it every Christmas season.

GRADE: A-

CONTENT OVERVIEW: There's nothing inappropriate here. A woman holds a priest's hand and looks at him longingly; he leaves.

MESSAGES TO DISCUSS: The best way to serve God is through serving others (Mosiah 2:17). We can choose to not lose hope and faith by putting our trust in the Lord (Joel 3:16); this faith and hope leads to good works (Ether 12:4).

SINGIN' IN THE RAIN (G, 1952)

Gene Kelly, Debbie Reynolds, and Donald O'Connor star in this infectiously joyous musical about a silent movie star who must adapt to avoid becoming obsolete with the invention of "talkies." In addition to having some of the best song-and-dance numbers ever captured on screen (the choreography is stunning), the actors charm, the comedy hits its target, and the story is a lot of fun. A wonderful film for all ages.

GRADE: A+

CONTENT OVERVIEW: There is some smoking, a staged fistfight during the filming of a movie, and a mildly sensual number with dancing girls in costumes that show some leg (though being made in the 1950s, it's all very mild and innocent by today's standards).

MESSAGES TO DISCUSS: Whatever you choose to do for a career, do it with integrity and dignity (Ephesians 4:28; Colossians 3:23). All secrets come out sooner or later (Luke 8:17).

SOUL SURFER (PG, 2011)

Soul Surfer is based on the true story of Bethany Hamilton, a teen surfing prodigy who lost an arm in a tiger shark attack. The film overcomes a generous sprinkling of sports-movie clichés through the strength of its acting, the power of the story, and the sincerity of its message. The script is fairly solid, though some lines of dialogue are a bit hackneyed and the inclusion of a fictional arch-rival is unnecessary. Still, the film sticks mostly to incredible facts, impressive surfing footage, and lovely music while unabashedly emphasizing strong families and faith in Jesus Christ.

GRADE: B+

CONTENT ADVISORY: Men and teenage boys wear swimming trunks, while women and teenage girls wear bikinis and short shorts, but this is accurate to the surfing culture in Hawaii and not gratuitous or sensualized. A brief shark attack and its traumatic aftermath are realistically portrayed, with some blood and quick views of an arm stump, but the film doesn't linger on gore. The scene is likely too intense for young children, however.

MESSAGES TO DISCUSS: The Lord gives, and He takes away (Job 1:21). Parents who lovingly and supportively raise their children to follow Jesus will likely see them follow Him forever (Proverbs 22:6).

We can do all things through Christ, who strengthens us (Philippians 4:13). Learn in your youth to follow God (Alma 37:35). Love is the greatest power (Moroni 7:46–47). We cannot see, at the present time, the glory and blessings the Lord has prepared for us after our difficulties (Doctrine and Covenants 58:3–4).

SOUND OF MUSIC, THE (G, 1965)

With stunning footage of the Swiss alps, unforgettable songs, and a seminal performance by Julie Andrews, *Sound of Music* is rightfully regarded as one of the finest musicals ever made. Andrews stars as a postulant (candidate to become a nun) who takes a post as a governess for a widower and his children. She helps the unhappy family rediscover the joys of living and love, until the rise of the Nazis threatens everything they've built together. This is inspiring filmmaking at its best.

GRADE: A+

CONTENT OVERVIEW: Some smoking and drinking. A character is threatened at gunpoint. There are a few chaste kisses.

MESSAGES TO DISCUSS: We cannot run from our problems; we must face them (Proverbs 28:1). God always provides a way for us to do his will and find happiness, even in our trials (1 Nephi 3:7; 2 Nephi 2:25). Marriage is ordained of God (1 Corinthians 11:11).

SPECIAL WITNESSES OF CHRIST (NR, 1999)

This well-made film finds the modern prophets and apostles testifying of the Savior from various sacred sites around the world (Elder Holland in Gethsemane, President Hinckley in the Sacred Grove and the Garden Tomb, Elder Faust in Nauvoo, and so on). The film gives audiences the chance to hear the testimonies of living servants of God. It's stirring and inspiring.

GRADE: A

CONTENT OVERVIEW: There's nothing offensive here.

MESSAGES TO DISCUSS: Salvation comes only through Jesus Christ (John 14:6; Mosiah 3:17). God works through prophets and apostles (Amos 3:7; Ephesians 2:19–20).

STAR WARS: EPISODE I—THE PHANTOM MENACE (PG, 1999)

Writer director George Lucas's return to the *Star Wars* saga sixteen years after *Return of the Jedi* was far from triumphant. This first in a prequel trilogy tracking Anakin Skywalker's rise and fall has stale dialogue, some wooden acting, and a plodding pace, though leads Liam Neeson and Ewan McGregor do their best with what they're given. Jar Jar Binks is inexcusable. Still, as a sheer spectacle it delights with a stellar lightsaber duel and a thrilling pod race reminiscent of the chariot race in *Ben-Hur*. *The Phantom Menace* stumbles frequently, but it sets the stage for future installments.

GRADE: C+

CONTENT OVERVIEW: It contains no foul language, sex, nudity, or substance abuse. There is plenty of bloodless fantasy violence (laser shootouts, etc), mostly directed at robots, though (spoiler) a man is cut in half and another is stabbed in the stomach during a lightsaber duel (both bloodless)

MESSAGES TO DISCUSS: To overcome fear we sometimes translate it into the false power of anger, which anger then leads to hate, which hate leads to suffering (Moroni 9:5). Curiously it is perfect love, that is, self-sacrifice for another, that most effectively casts out fear (1 John 4:18, Moroni 8:16) a concept that this series explores much later in *Return of the Jedi*.

STAR WARS: EPISODE II—ATTACK OF THE CLONES (PG, 2002)

This second Star Wars prequel is often remembered for its atrociously hammy romantic dialogue, but the story itself is pretty solid, as Obi-Wan Kenobi unveils a plot to overthrow the Republic, clone troopers are brought in to defend it, and Anakin Skywalker and Padme Amidala fall for each other (even as the former starts his journey toward the dark side of the Force). Though the first half has some pacing issues, the second displays plenty of action and excitement, some dazzling visuals, and some well-played nostalgia. The series's sense of fun starts to return here. George Lucas may not be an exemplary writer, but his creativity in creating worlds and creatures is unparalleled. Plus, fans get to see Yoda finally step into action.

GRADE: B

CONTENT OVERVIEW: There is plentiful action violence (laser blasts, lightsaber duels, attacks by giant animals), but it's bloodless and in a sci-fi fantasy context. Padme wears several outfits that reveal her midriff.

MESSAGES TO DISCUSS: Hatred, violence, and revenge are not justified, no matter the circumstances (1 Peter 3:9); they will destroy your soul. A child's mind is a wonderful thing; we'd do well to emulate their innocence and honesty (Mosiah 3:19). Arrogance can blind us to our weaknesses; humility can help us to turn them into strengths (Ether 12:27).

STAR WARS: EPISODE III—REVENGE OF THE SITH (PG-13, 2005)

This is the darkest and most violent Star Wars film, dealing as it does with Anakin Skywalker's descent into the dark side of the Force, becoming Darth Vader, and helping Emperor Palpatine to wipe out the Jedi. This is a heartbreaking film, but it's also action-packed and utterly engrossing as a breathlessly paced epic tragedy that's easily the best of the prequels. Though there are still some stumbles with screenwriting and acting, even those have improved notably here. The film sets up the original trilogy perfectly, and John Williams's musical score here is one of his best ever.

GRADE: B+

CONTENT OVERVIEW: As Darth Vader, Anakin goes on a violent (though bloodless) killing spree, assisted by clone troopers. Jedi are gunned down by laser blasts, while aliens and robots are slashed by lightsaber. Anakin even kills Jedi children (to keep them from growing up to oppose the Empire), though thankfully this occurs off screen. All of this is portrayed as tragic and heartbreaking, not as glorified violence. Anakin strangles his pregnant wife with the Force; she later gives birth to Luke and Leia before she passes away. Palpatine morphs into the hideous Emperor as his lightning blasts are deflected back to him. Anakin's legs are cut off in a duel with Obi-Wan Kenobi; he rolls next to a lava river and ignites on fire, becoming badly burned. This incident leads to the necessity of the mechanical suit he wears to survive as Darth Vader.

MESSAGES TO DISCUSS: Wickedness never was happiness (Alma 41:10). Beware those who speak flattering words and appeal to your ego (Mosiah 26:6), and those who call evil good, and good evil (Isaiah 5:20–21).

STAR WARS: EPISODE IV—A NEW HOPE (PG, 1977)

The one that started it all (originally released simply as *Star Wars*), this film is loaded with iconic characters, classic moments, incredible music, and then-groundbreaking visual effects, even if it's a bit slowly paced and sometimes hammily acted by today's standards. Luke Skywalker joins with Han Solo, Chewbacca, Obi-Wan Kenobi, C-3PO, and R2-D2 to rescue Princess Leia, battle Darth Vader, and join the rebellion in destroying the Death Star.

GRADE: A-

CONTENT OVERVIEW: Some people are shot with lasers. The Death Star blows up an entire planet, killing millions (though we don't see their deaths). Obi-Wan sacrifices himself and disappears when slashed with a lightsaber. There are a few mild profanities.

MESSAGES TO DISCUSS: Like Luke uses the Force, we can follow the guidance of the Holy Ghost to know how to act; it will magnify our own capabilities (Doctrine and Covenants 11:12–13). Those who follow fools are equally foolish (Helaman 13:29).

STAR WARS: EPISODE V—THE EMPIRE STRIKES BACK (PG, 1980)

I love all the Star Wars movies, but this is the only one where they absolutely perfected the formula. George Lucas produces while a superior writer (Lawrence Kasdan) and a superior director (Irvin Kershner) work out the details. The Empire lashes out at the Rebellion for the events of the previous film. Han and Leia's bickering chemistry is a wonderful exercise in unsentimental romance while Luke's training with Yoda is loaded with meaningful truths. Also, Darth Vader has never been more awesomely imposing. Asteroid chases, abominable snowmen, a city in the clouds, and (spoiler) Vader revealing himself as Luke's father are particular highlights.

GRADE: A+

CONTENT OVERVIEW: Vader slices off Luke's hand with a lightsaber (no blood). Space battles with ships colliding and exploding, lightsaber duels, and laser blasts are all par for the course here. Vader uses the Force to strangle officers he's displeased with. Han and Leia kiss.

MESSAGES TO DISCUSS: There are no miracles without belief (Moroni 7:35–37; Mormon 9:19–20). Vengeance, fear, and anger are not righteous (3 Nephi 11:29–30); the path to wickedness is easier and quicker. The difference is discernible (Moroni 7:15–17); the "good side" (the Holy Ghost) speaks peace to our minds and hearts (Galatians 5:22–23).

STAR WARS: EPISODE VI—RETURN OF THE JEDI (PG, 1983)

The finale of the original trilogy finds our heroes rescuing Han Solo from the clutches of Jabba the Hut, the Rebellion waging their last campaign against the evil Empire, and Luke making a desperate last attempt to help his father find redemption. Though it's not as strongly written as *Empire*, there's a great deal of action and emotional payoff here. Some may take issue with the Ewoks (I never have), but it's hard not to be moved when Luke's altruism and courage awaken a spirit of repentance in Darth Vader/Anakin.

GRADE: A-

CONTENT OVERVIEW: Princess Leia wears a "slave outfit" that resembles a gold bikini after she's captured by Jabba the Hut. Luke is electrocuted by the Emperor almost to the point of death but is rescued by his father, who perishes from being electrocuted himself while saving his son and destroying the Emperor. The space battles, duels, and laser gunfights that are typical of this series are present here, though it's all bloodless. A giant monster bites the head off of a pig-like creature.

MESSAGES TO DISCUSS: When children's hearts are turned toward their parents (Malachi 4:6), they can inspire their parents to be repent (1 Nephi 16:20–24) which brings honor to the parents (Exodus 20:12). Anger and aggression lead to evil (3 Nephi 11:29–30).

STATE FAIR (NR, 1945)

This breezy and whimsical Rogers and Hammerstein musical finds a farming family headed to the state fair. The parents enter baking and animal competitions, while the maturing children get their first taste of romance with sweethearts they meet during the festivities. It's all a bit hokey and lightweight, but fans of old movies will enjoy the characters, revel in the songs, and wax nostalgic for a bygone era.

GRADE: B

CONTENT OVERVIEW: A man spends time alone with a woman in her hotel room, but nothing inappropriate is implied. An old man asks his wife if she wants to see a burlesque show (the dancing girls come out and do a mildly sensual dance routine). A man finds out the woman he's been romancing is already married and breaks of the relationship.

MESSAGES TO DISCUSS: Men and woman are meant to be together (1 Corinthians 11:11). "Successful marriages and families are established and maintained on principles of faith, prayer, repentance, forgiveness, respect, love, compassion, work, and wholesome recreational activities" ("The Family: A Proclamation to the World," *Ensign*, Nov. 1995, 102).

STATES OF GRACE (PG-13, 2005)

Most Christmas movies have nothing to do with Jesus Christ, but *States of Grace* helps to fill that gap. Wrongfully subtitled *God's Army 2* in certain markets, it's actually a stand-alone film. It's a broadly Christian tale that happens to feature two Latter-day Saint missionaries, along with a Pentecostal preacher, an actress raised in a Christian household, and a repentant gangbanger. The film isn't for everyone. It explores with heartbreaking depth the bitter sorrow of sin, to the point that I know of some viewers who didn't finish the film and thus missed out on its entire message that we all need redemption, which comes through the Savior's loving sacrifice for us. Well-acted, well-written, and like most great morality tales, it brings audiences down before lifting them higher than ever.

GRADE: A

CONTENT OVERVIEW: *States of Grace* earns its rating with intense depictions of gang violence and tastefully handled, yet nevertheless mature, subject matter. Several quick shots of women in bikinis, though realistically establishing the film's Southern California setting, are arguably unnecessary.

MESSAGES TO DISCUSS: All of us sin and fall short of the glory of God (Romans 3:23). Redemption comes through the sacrifice and grace of the Messiah (Jesus Christ), to all who have a broken heart and a contrite spirit (2 Nephi 2:6–8). Though our sins be as scarlet, they may be white as snow (Isaiah 1:18). Converted souls renounce their violent ways (Alma 24). We should be careful not to judge (Matthew 7:1–5) but rather to inspire righteousness through love (Matthew 9:10–13; Luke 7:36–50). "Some will make critically serious mistakes. . . . You can be washed clean through the atoning sacrifice of the Savior Jesus Christ. You may in times of trouble think that you are not worth saving because you have made mistakes, big or little, and you think you are now lost. That is *never* true!" (Elder Boyd K. Packer, "Counsel to Youth," *Ensign*, Nov. 2011).

STORIES FROM THE LIFE OF PORTER ROCKWELL (NR, 2010)

Much like the man it reveals, Covenant Communications's new documentary *Stories from the Life of Porter Rockwell* emerges with glaring imperfections but is ultimately redeemed by things done right. Featuring insights and commentary by a variety of well-respected LDS history scholars, the film attempts to strike a balanced portrayal of a man some called a murderer, others a hero. The film attempts to, and mostly succeeds at, showing the whole man, with his strengths and weaknesses, virtues and vices on display. On two things, it seems, all of the scholars in the film agree: Porter loved Joseph Smith and Porter was an excellent marksman. As for the film itself, Richard Purdy is perfectly cast as Rockwell. He possesses a gritty integrity that makes him perfect for the role. The other actors, however, are a mixed bag. In many cases not enough care was taken, either in the casting or in the wardrobe and makeup, to make them appear of the time period portrayed. Of course, once the Saints arrive in Utah, all of the locations are more authentic. On the other hand, the cinematography is gorgeous to look at in many cases, and the musical score, while not what I would've expected, is memorable and well-utilized. For history buffs or those interested in learning more about this truly fascinating figure, the film is a recommended purchase.

GRADE: B-

CONTENT OVERVIEW: Gunfights are portrayed, though not bloodily.

MESSAGES TO DISCUSS: "At [Porter's] funeral service, Elder Joseph F. Smith of the Council of the Twelve said, 'He had his little faults, but Porter's life on earth, taken altogether, was one worthy of example, and reflected honor upon the Church. Through all his trials he had never once forgotten his obligations to his brethren and his God.'" (Lawrence Cummins, "Orrin Porter Rockwell," *Friend*, May 1984).

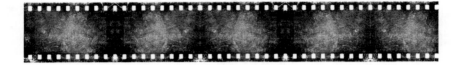

SURF'S UP (PG, 2007)

This computer-animated family film about surfing penguins is underrated and underseen. It has a fun story, great voiceover work (Shia LaBeouf, Zooey Deschanel, Jeff Bridges, James Woods, and Latter-day Saint actor Jon Heder are among the cast), and brilliantly rendered tropical locations and surfing action. *Surf's Up* has a documentary feel; a camera crew follows a cocky arctic penguin as he learns humility and heroism from his mentor upon entering the world's premiere surfing competition. The witty screenplay is the film's strongest asset, amusing both kids and adults.

GRADE: B

CONTENT OVERVIEW: Some name-calling, one mild profanity, a pair of mild innuendos that'll go over kids' heads, and the implication that a penguin pees on another to cure the sting of a sea urchin.

MESSAGES TO DISCUSS: We are to love our neighbors as ourselves, putting their needs before our own (Galatians 5:14). The proud will be made humble, whereas humility leads to the kind of success that matters (Luke 14:11; Philippians 2:3).

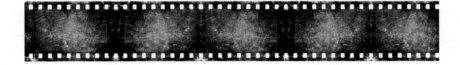

SWISS FAMILY ROBINSON (G, 1960)

Disney's live-action adaptation of the classic novel is the stuff of child-hood fantasy, with the shipwrecked European family taming jungle animals, battling pirates, and building an immaculate mansion of a tree house, as the two eldest brothers fight over a beautiful tomboy they rescued. The film is a delightful adventure with a noble emphasis on familial solidarity, not to mention some spectacular footage.

GRADE: A-

CONTENT OVERVIEW: There are a few kisses. A tiger attempts to attack a young boy but is fended off, while a battle with pirates sees the villains shot and felled by booby traps.

MESSAGES TO DISCUSS: Parents should teach their children not to fight, but to love and serve one another (Mosiah 4:14–15). Men and women should marry for love and have children to ensure that family lines continue (1 Nephi 7:1).

SWORD IN THE STONE, THE (G, 1963)

This animated Disney film is a version of the early years of the Arthur legend, as the future king (here a young boy) endures ridicule from his uncle and cousin and is trained by the wizard Merlin to be a benevolent, courageous, and wise ruler. Along the way, Arthur observes magical duels and learns life lessons firsthand from the animal kingdom as Merlin turns him into a squirrel, a fish, and a bird. It all culminates with Arthur pulling Excalibur from its lodging place in a rock when nobody else can, resulting in his coronation. Above all, the film is loads of fun with a terrific sense of humor and marvelous jazz music.

GRADE: A

CONTENT OVERVIEW: Arthur is imperiled various times, but the tone is such that only the very smallest of children run any risk of being afraid. Female squirrels kiss men who've been turned into squirrels, much to the chagrin of the latter. An evil witch turns herself into a lovely maiden, shaking her behind and her shoulders, before transforming back into an old hag.

MESSAGES TO DISCUSS: Males and females, by divine design, are meant to be paired together (Genesis 2:24). It is good to be learned, but wisdom comes only if knowledge is paired with virtue (2 Nephi 9:28–29).

TANGLED (PG, 2010)

Easily the best non-Pixar Disney animated film of the past decade, *Tangled* instantly joins the ranks (alongside *The Lion King, Aladdin, Beauty and the Beast, Tarzan,* and *The Emperor's New Groove*) of modern animated classics from the studio and represents a return to form for the Mouse House. This update of the Rapunzel story is sentimental (in the best way) and energizes the tired "princess story" template with stunning animation, catchy songs from Oscar-winner Alan Menken, and a solid sense of humor. Utterly charming to the point that my wife and brother-in-law, neither of whom are huge fans of this genre, both enjoyed it a lot.

GRADE: A

CONTENT OVERVIEW: Language and innuendo are non-existent, though animated slapstick violence might be a concern for parents of small children, who might imitate what they see. A young man is stabbed in a more serious scene (we see no blood and he's saved). There are a few kisses.

MESSAGES TO DISCUSS: No matter what your past, you can change and be a better person (Isaiah 1:18).

TARZAN (G, 1999)

Disney's animated take on the classic Edgar Rice Burroughs story boasts expert voiceover work, "tree-surfing" action (a dazzling hybrid of hand-drawn and computer animation), a bold telling of the story, memorable characters, and an excellent soundtrack by Phil Collins. Orphaned in the jungle, Tarzan is raised by apes until manhood, when he encounters Jane, her father, and a deceptive gamesman. This is one of Disney's best modern animated films.

GRADE: A-

CONTENT OVERVIEW: Tarzan's parents and a gorilla baby are both murdered by a jaguar, though neither event occurs on screen. Tarzan fights that jaguar to the death later on, killing it off screen while defending his gorilla family (he hoists its carcass over his head after the fact). Gorillas and people are kidnapped and threatened. A villain accidentally hangs himself to death while cutting through vines (we see the silhouette of his shadow, nothing more). Throughout the film, Tarzan wears nothing but a loincloth, exposing his muscular torso and legs in full.

MESSAGES TO DISCUSS: Adoptive families are capable of love and connection equal to that of blood families (2 Nephi 1:30–32). Men and women are meant to be together (1 Corinthians 11:11).

TEN COMMANDMENTS, THE (G, 1956)

Winner of seven Academy Awards, including Best Picture, this Cecille B. Demille masterpiece finds Charlton Heston as the quintessential screen Moses, Yul Brynner as the imposing pharaoh, and a cast of thousands of extras bringing the Exodus story to life. Impressive sets, a reverent tone, and legendary filmmaking make this classic worth multiple viewings.

GRADE: A-

CONTENT OVERVIEW: There are some whippings and a stabbings with very little blood (this was the 1950s, after all). Israelites drink wine and dance somewhat sensually at the foot of Sinai; Moses comes down and delivers the word of the Lord to them.

MESSAGES TO DISCUSS: Parents may want to use this film as a springboard to study the book of Exodus in the Old Testament, where this story is found. Israel was led out of Egypt and blessed according to their faith and obedience, and hindered according to their unbelief and disobedience; they were led to the land of promise by the Lord (1 Nephi 17:23–35).

TESTAMENTS OF ONE FOLD AND ONE SHEPHERD, THE (NR, 2000)

This seventy-minute film was produced by the Church and enjoyed an extended run at the Legacy Theatre on Temple Square. It portrays events from the life of Christ interwoven with concurrent events in the New World. The dialogue can be a little awkward at times, but the beauty of the filmmaking, the power of the acting, the truthfulness of the story, and the clarity with which this film displays the relationship between the Bible and the Book of Mormon, all combine for a powerhouse viewing experience every time. Rick Macy in particular, as the Nephite father Helam, gives a magnetic performance. Great cinematography and music highlight this majestic film, which displays love for Jesus Christ on every frame.

GRADE: A-

CONTENT OVERVIEW: There is a chaste kiss. Jesus Christ is scourged, a crown of thorns is placed on His head, and He's crucified. Earthquakes and fires in the New World accompany the Lord's crucifixion.

MESSAGES TO DISCUSS: The Lord Jesus Christ was born of a virgin (Alma 7:10). He is the Messiah, sent to teach the way back to God, to heal the sick, to atone for the sins of the world, and to bring to pass the universal resurrection (Mosiah 3:5–12). His death caused great calamity and destruction in the New World (3 Nephi 8). He appeared in resurrected form to the Nephites, teaching them the gospel, ordaining Apostles, blessing the children, and healing the sick (3 Nephi 11, 17).

THOR (PG-13, 2011)

The Norse god of thunder as a superhero is a silly idea, even for comic books, but in the capable hands of director Kenneth Branagh, *Thor* strikes a nice tonal balance between Shakespearean drama and epic popcorn entertainment. The cast is excellent and the screenplay solid. I still think the wardrobe looks silly, especially when the gods descend to earth, but the film wisely has a sense of humor about this. Though Thor's character arc would've had more weight (and his romance been more meaningful) had he spent more than a few days on earth, the film has a good pace and never bores. The action is thrilling, the characters are memorable, the romance chastely crackles, and the one-liners hit their marks.

GRADE: B+

CONTENT ADVISORY: There is some action violence, though not gory or especially gratuitous. There are a few mild profanities. Two characters drink beer. There is no sexuality or nudity; a Norse god is briefly seen shirtless and two women gaze longingly. Characters known as "ice gods" may be frightening for children.

MESSAGES TO DISCUSS: Though Thor is fiction (as are his powers), the film contemplates a correct principle: True miracles and godly power are wholly compatible with true science. Brigham Young taught:

> It is hard to get the people to believe that God is a scientific character, that He lives by science or strict law, that by this He is, and by law He was made what He is; and will remain to all eternity because of His faithful adherence to law. It is a most difficult thing to make the people believe that every art and science and all wisdom come from Him, and that He is their Author. (*Journal of Discourses*, vol. 13, p. 302, Nov. 13 1870)

There are parallels between the fictional Thor's journey and our own. We have both been sent to earth by our fathers to learn humility, peacemaking, and selflessness (Abraham 3:22–25). God chastens us out of love, for our profit, that we may return and receive glory from him (Deuteronomy 8:2–3; Hebrews 12:9–10; Doctrine and Covenants 95:1). There is no greater love than to be willing to die for one's friends (John 15:13).

TO THIS END WAS I BORN (NR, 1993)

In my opinion, this is the best movie the Church has ever produced. In a half an hour, it tells the story of the final week of the Savior's life, including the Last Supper, the Atonement, the Lord's visit to the spirit world, and the Resurrection. It's perfect for Easter, with gorgeous music, solid production values, purposeful direction, and a reverent depiction of the Lord. A shorter version, called *The Lamb of God*, is also available, but this is the one to get.

GRADE: A+

CONTENT OVERVIEW: Jesus Christ is mocked, hit, scourged, a crown of thorns is placed on his head, and he's crucified.

MESSAGES TO DISCUSS: The Lord Jesus Christ is the Messiah. He was sent to teach the way back to God, to heal the sick, to atone for the sins of the world, and to bring to pass the universal Resurrection (Mosiah 3:5–12).

TOY STORY (G, 1995)

Disney-Pixar's groundbreaking film was the first feature-length computer-animated film, and it still impresses today, not just visually, but with its clever, heartwarming, and wonderfully funny screenplay. Cowboy action figure Woody (Tom Hanks, in fine form) is the leader of the toys in Andy's bedroom until the clueless and vain space toy Buzz Lightyear (Tim Allen, also great) unwittingly steals the spotlight.

GRADE: A

CONTENT OVERVIEW: A bully child blows toys up with explosives; he also mixes and matches their body parts to create creepy "mutant toys" (who end up being good-natured). A dog bites into an alien doll.

MESSAGES TO DISCUSS: We must be careful not to judge others based on their appearance and our first impressions (1 Samuel 16:7). One of the greatest things we can do is bring joy to children (3 Nephi 17:21–23).

TOY STORY 2 (G, 1999)

This sequel pulls off the rare feat of surpassing the original, as Woody is kidnapped (toy-napped?) by a collector, learning of his identity as the star of a Howdy Doody–type cowboy show in the 1950s and meeting horse Bullseye, cowgirl Jessie (Joan Cusack), and old prospector Stinky Pete along the way. His friends embark on a crosstown journey in an attempt to rescue him. The level of detail in the animation is impressive, as is the screenplay, which is jam-packed with pathos, witty dialogue, and clever homages to various cinematic genres.

GRADE: A+

CONTENT OVERVIEW: In a moment of alarm, a Mr. Potato Head's back end opens up, emptying its contents (mimicking defecation). A toy punches another toy and tears the stitching on his arm apart. Toys are placed in various perilous and chaotic situations.

MESSAGES TO DISCUSS: Happiness comes from putting the needs of others before our own (Matthew 23:11). Friends come to one another's rescue (Doctrine and Covenants 134:11).

TOY STORY 3 (G, 2010)

Toy Story 3 continues the franchise's tradition of telling stories that tap into the sense of wonder and imagination in adults and children alike. Like all of Pixar's movies, the characters, comedy, and storytelling brim with more ingenuity, wit, and heart than nearly anything else on the market. Pixar doesn't just make great children's films or great family films, they make great films, period. Like the studio's *Up, Toy Story 3* explores poignant themes of aging and mortality while wowing audiences with thrilling adventure and humor that puts competitors to shame. It is as charming as the first two films, with the advantage of ten years' advancement in computer animation and a screenplay that is truly touching. Highly recommended for the whole family (except the youngest of children; there is a slightly darker and more menacing tone and our heroes are put in grave peril, which may frighten or disturb them).

GRADE: A

CONTENT OVERVIEW: All of the central characters find themselves sliding to their apparent demise in a trash dump incinerator. When escape seems impossible, they resolutely hold on to one another to face death. Though they are (spoiler) rescued at the last second, it's a surprisingly heavy moment that may prove too intense for young children.

MESSAGES TO DISCUSS: If we bring happiness and comfort to others, we are fulfilling our purpose for existing (Mosiah 18:8–10). We can face death courageously if we have loved and are loved (1 John 4:18).

TREASURE IN HEAVEN: THE JOHN TANNER STORY (NR, 2009)

Director T. C. Christensen (*17 Miracles*), as well as his talented cast and crew, has captured with wonderful detail the story of one of Church history's unsung heroes. As in *Only a Stonecutter*, he does so in about twenty minutes; perfect for family home evenings with youth who have short attention spans. John Tanner was a well-to-do New Yorker in the 1830s who experienced a crippling illness, as well as a meeting with missionaries, which affected his life and the Church forever. To divulge any detail would be to rob the viewer of enjoying the story as it unfolds. Suffice it to say that the tale is one of consecration and wholehearted dedication to the Lord as Tanner exercises faith in God's promises. Becoming a major hero for the Church, and much beloved by the Prophet Joseph, his tale carries a rich power in and of itself, a power fully realized in this screen adaptation. The acting is very good. Nathan Mitchell, who has portrayed Joseph Smith for the better part of a decade, continues to impress as the Prophet of the Restoration. Matthew Maddox and Shauna Thompson, respectively, portray John Tanner and his wife, Elizabeth, and both do inspiring, realistic work. The music, the cinematography, the creativity of the editing, and the screenplay, all are top notch and effective. All that said, this is not to say this is an epic masterpiece, and nor was it meant to be. It's a simple, faith-affirming tale, and well-told. Worth the purchase, both for the quality of the product and for the probability that more films like this will be made if we support them.

GRADE: A-

CONTENT OVERVIEW: A bloody and infected leg wound is shown.

MESSAGES TO DISCUSS: For every sacrifice we make, the Lord rewards us a hundredfold and more (Mark 10:29–30). What we have has been given us by the Lord; we have no right to withhold our substance from others (Mosiah 4:21).

ULTIMATE GIFT, THE (PG, 2006)

The Ultimate Gift tries, for the most part successfully, to be many things at once: Christian drama, romance, coming-of-age morality tale, and adventure. It nails the first three, and though the fourth feels a little forced, the final product is an involving, well-acted movie that is definitely worth your time. A vain young man is left an inheritance from a recently deceased rich relative (James Garner), who requires him to perform a series of character-building tasks before he can acquire it. It's funny and touching, with a great cast including Abigail Breslin and Brian Dennehy.

GRADE: B+

CONTENT OVERVIEW: Some mild profanity. A man is struck and soldiers threaten to shoot him.

MESSAGES TO DISCUSS: It profits us nothing to gain possessions if we lose our souls; we must lose ourselves in service to God and others

(Mark 8:35–36). If we seek riches, we should do so to help the poor (Jacob 2:18–19).

UP (PG, 2009)

Disney-Pixar's *Up* interweaves its adventure and belly laughs with surprisingly tender expressions of marital devotion and loyal friendship. The film possesses an innocence, and ultimately a sweetness, that was pleasing to my soul. The story revolves around elderly widower Carl Fredricksen, who is facing eviction from the home in which he made a lifetime of memories with his recently departed (and much beloved) wife. Rather than allow that to happen, the aging balloon vendor ties thousands of inflated helium orbs to his home and flies away with it, steering his house toward an adventurous destination he and his wife had always dreamed of visiting but never did. Much to Carl's surprise, his adorably precocious neighbor Russell (who is a type of Boy Scout) has accidentally tagged along for the ride. The wise yet cantankerous elder and the naïve but loving child become unlikely friends while facing danger in the style of classic Hollywood serial adventures, complete with stunning locales, dangerous animals, dastardly villains, and a *literal* dogfight centered around a zeppelin thousands of feet in the air (you'll see). While *Up* is pure fantasy, its emotional center is firmly grounded and this is the film's greatest strength. While on the surface the film may be about thrills, laughs, and adventure, such is merely the canvas on which the filmmakers explore love, loss, healing, and finding joy in our relationships with those around us.

GRADE: A+

CONTENT OVERVIEW: A man strikes another man on the head with a walker, drawing minor blood. It is implied that an elderly man loses his wife to old age or illness (we see her in a hospital bed, then see him at the funeral). There are numerous scenes featuring a man, boy, and dog in peril. Dogs fall to their supposed deaths, as does a villain.

MESSAGES TO DISCUSS: We can work through our grief by loving and serving others. After tribulation come blessings (Doctrine and Covenants 58:2–4).

WALL-E (G, 2008)

A wonderful family film, a Charlie Chaplin–style romantic comedy, and one of the decade's boldest sci-fi stories all rolled into one, *Wall-E* is yet another filmmaking triumph from Disney-Pixar. Lonely robot Wall-E spends his days cleaning up the over-polluted and abandoned earth until he meets the lovely female reconnaissance drone Eve, who has come to examine whether the planet is again able to sustain human life. Their (charmingly romantic) adventures lead them to a massive spaceship filled with what's left of the human race, obese and naïve from centuries of overindulgence. Together, they fight to reach their—and mankind's—potential.

GRADE: A

CONTENT OVERVIEW: There is some slapstick violence, and, in a more harrowing moment, the title character "dies" (is broken and loses power), though he's repaired and "comes back to life."

MESSAGES TO DISCUSS: Mankind has a stewardship over the planet and a responsibility to take good care of God's creations (Doctrine and Covenants 49:19; Moses 1:28–32; Doctrine and Covenants 104:17; 89:11–12; 49:21), including our mortal bodies (Doctrine and Covenants 89; 1 Corinthians 3:16–17).

WAR HORSE (PG-13, 2011)

A gorgeous Spielberg adaptation of a stage play of the same name, *War Horse* captures both the sorrows of war and the sympathies of humanity. It has both intimate storytelling and an epic scale reminiscent of old Hollywood classics such as *Gone with the Wind* and *Lawrence of Arabia*. Wisely, though the horse is treated as a central character, it's also a narrative device to explore the human condition in response to war. Following the animal from owner to owner throughout World War I, we're given a host of memorable characters to connect with and care about as the film examines the courage, terror, brutality, and compassion of people who know that their lives may end at any time. Lush cinematography, fine attention to historical detail in wardrobe and sets, a stirring score by longtime Spielberg composer John Williams, and solid performances highlight this tale. It runs too long and some elements of the plot are too coincidental, but these flaws detract very little from a film of this quality.

GRADE: B+

CONTENT OVERVIEW: There are few mild profanities. There are several scenes of intense battlefield violence (shootings and stabbings, though none are graphic or particularly bloody). We see the corpses of soldiers and horses. A scene, difficult to watch, portrays a panicked horse getting caught in barbed wire. There is no sexuality, nudity, or crude humor.

MESSAGES TO DISCUSS: "Animals . . . occupy an assigned sphere and play an eternal role in the great plan of creation, redemption, and salvation" (Bruce R. McConkie, "Animals," *Mormon Doctrine* [2nd ed. Salt Lake City: Bookcraft, 1966], 29).

"Men must become harmless before the brute creation . . . lose their vicious dispositions, and cease to destroy the animal race . . . unless it [becomes] necessary in order to preserve [themselves] from hunger" (*Teachings of the Prophet Joseph Smith*, p. 71). War leads some to become callous and cruel, while it inspires compassion, faith, and humility in others (Alma 62:41).

WE BELIEVE IN CHRIST (NR, 1995)

This thirty-minute film, narrated by Elder Jeffrey R. Holland, was produced by the Church as a missionary fireside to share our beliefs about the Savior. Between Elder Holland's teachings and testimony, music by the Mormon Tabernacle Choir, modern vignettes depicting members overcoming trials by turning to the Lord, and gorgeous footage re-creating events from the ministry of Christ in the Holy Land and in the Americas, this is a wonderful choice for family home evening or to share with those not of our faith.

GRADE: A

CONTENT OVERVIEW: Jesus is scourged and crucified.

MESSAGES TO DISCUSS: "We talk of Christ, we rejoice in Christ, we preach of Christ, we prophesy of Christ, and we write according to our prophecies, that our children may know to what source they make look for a remission of their sins" (2 Nephi 25:26). Those who read the Book of Mormon, ponder it, and pray about it in faith will receive a witness by the Holy Ghost that it is true (Moroni 10:3–5).

WE BOUGHT A ZOO (PG, 2011)

Director Cameron Crowe brings his love of quirky characters, left-field humor, and light rock music to family filmmaking with *We Bought a Zoo*, an engaging and inspiring true story about a widower and his children who see a fresh start by, you guessed it, buying an old run-down zoo. It's a tale of loss, heartache, and familial healing through forgiveness and the forming of new friendships. It's tremendously moving. It's funny. It's romantic. It's got terrific acting, predictably by Matt Damon, but also by Scarlett Johansson, who dials down the glamour and gives her most down-to-earth and likable performance here. The supporting characters are all great fun. Sometimes Crowe's affinity for music montages bogs down the pace, but overall this is a film that made me want to nurture and treasure my relationships and left a smile on my face.

GRADE: A-

CONTENT OVERVIEW: There is no sexuality, crude humor, or violence. There's a fair amount of mild-to-moderate profanity for a PG-rated film, one uttered by a small child (repeating what she overheard elsewhere).

MESSAGES TO DISCUSS: We have to experience sorrow in order to grow and to appreciate joy (Doctrine and Covenants 29:39; 2 Nephi 2:11, Doctrine and Covenants 122:5–9, Doctrine and Covenants 58:3–4). "Successful marriages and families are established and maintained on principles of faith, prayer, repentance, forgiveness, respect, love, compassion, work, and wholesome recreational activities" ("The Family: A Proclamation to the World," *Ensign*, Nov. 1995, 102).

WHALE RIDER (PG-13, 2002)

A fascinating look into the beliefs of a South Pacific tribe, *Whale Rider* is truly amazing. Keisha Castle-Hughes (later to star in *The Nativity Story*) became the youngest woman to ever be nominated for Best Actress (she was thirteen) for her harrowing performance as a Kiwi chief's granddaughter in New Zealand who bucks against tradition in her attempts to claim her destiny and become the first female chief. This is an insightful family and cultural drama.

GRADE: A-

CONTENT OVERVIEW: A few crude references, a girl's back (from the waist up) is shown while bathing, but the scene is matter-of-fact, not sensual. Some dead whales are shown (no gore).

MESSAGES TO DISCUSS: Women and men are equal before the Lord (2 Nephi 26:33). Children are entitled to their family's support (Doctrine and Covenants 83:4).

WILLY WONKA AND THE CHOCOLATE FACTORY (G, 1971)

Gene Wilder gives a wonderfully dry and darkly hilarious performance in this family-friendly favorite. In this adaptation of the Roald Dahl novel, a young boy finds a golden ticket in a chocolate bar and tours, along with his grandfather and several other child-adult combinations, the factory of great candy-maker Willy Wonka. It is terrifically imaginative, with wonderful lessons for children on respect, selflessness, and humility.

GRADE: A

CONTENT OVERVIEW: Children seem to be imperiled (turned into a giant blueberry, shrunk down into a tiny size, sucked into a giant tube, etc.) but are later revealed to be just fine. During a boat ride down a tunnel, frightening images (spiders, millipedes, a chicken being decapitated) are projected onto the walls.

MESSAGES TO DISCUSS: We shouldn't waste time in fruitless pursuits (Doctrine and Covenants 60:13), such as overuse of media. Don't be a glutton (Proverbs 23:20–21). Honesty results in blessings (Luke 8:15).

WINNIE THE POOH (G, 2011)

Sadly overlooked, this newer Disney film is the best Pooh adventure since the 1977 original, nearly matching that film in charm. Highlights include simple, but lovely, hand-drawn animation, full-bodied voiceover work (some by the original actors, some by replacements if those actors are now deceased), and a very funny screenplay. The characters of the Hundred Acre Wood have a contest to see who can find Eeyore a new tail. Kids will love it, and adults will find it to be nostalgic fun.

GRADE: B+

CONTENT OVERVIEW: There's nothing offensive here.

MESSAGES TO DISCUSS: The greatest happiness comes from loving our friends and putting the needs of others before our own (John 15:12; Philippians 2:4).

WIZARD OF OZ, THE (G, 1939)

This brilliant film likely needs no introduction (especially with *Wicked* expanding on the mythology). This 1939 version is a masterpiece of Old Hollywood moviemaking. Dorothy Gale and her dog, Toto, are swept away in a tornado from Depression-era Kansas (in black and white) to the mythical land of Oz (in glorious Technicolor). She walks the Yellow Brick Road in search of the wizard who might get her home, joined by a scarecrow, a tin man, and a cowardly lion, and pursued by a wicked witch.

GRADE: A

CONTENT OVERVIEW: There are some threatening and frightening scenes (an ominous tornado, a melting witch), but nothing that families can't watch together.

MESSAGES TO DISCUSS: Brains, heart, courage, and teamwork are necessary to succeed (Doctrine and Covenants 64:34). All secrets will come to light (Luke 8:17). The power to do marvelous things is already within us (Doctrine and Covenants 58:27–28).

WON'T BACK DOWN (PG, 2012)

Using fictional characters to explore a variety of real-life challenges in America's public schools, *Won't Back Down* is, for the most part, an intelligent and balanced look at the issue. Rather than vilifying teachers or teachers' unions as a whole, it shines a light on the corruption and idleness that has seeped into the system. Viola Davis (*The Help*) and Maggie Gyllenhaal (*The Dark Knight*) impress as a pair of inner-city mothers fighting for school reform, while Holly Hunter, Rosie Perez, and Oscar Isaac (*The Nativity Story*) also do fine work. A few of the peripheral characters, sadly, come across as one-note villains (albeit ones whose motivations make sense), while the film can also be a bit too sanctimonious for its own good. Still, there's some nicely played drama here (a scene between Davis and her son toward the end is particularly touching) and the film's arguments are clearly delineated. Those who enjoy this film should have a look at the acclaimed documentary *Waiting for Superman*.

GRADE: B

CONTENT OVERVIEW: There are a few mild profanities and scenes of people drinking alcohol socially. There is no violence or sexuality.

MESSAGES TO DISCUSS: You can accomplish great things if you don't give up when it gets hard (Galatians 6:9). The Lord puts great stock in learning, studying, wisdom, and intelligence, and so should we (Doctrine and Covenants 88:118; 130:18–19). There is no shame in having a learning disability; those who seek to help such individuals should focus on loving instead of judging, displaying acceptance, giving personal time and attention to work together, modify teaching styles, and more (see Laurie Wilson Thornton's excellent *Ensign* article "The Hidden Handicap" for more information [Apr. 1990]).

WORK AND THE GLORY TRILOGY, THE

The Work and the Glory (PG, 2004)
The Work and the Glory: American Zion (PG-13, 2005)
The Work and the Glory: A House Divided (PG, 2006)

Sadly, only the first three novels of Gerald Lund's celebrated Church historical fiction series were made into films. Thus, the story of the Restoration is just getting started when the film trilogy ends, though the story of the fictional Steed family gets a nice rounded arch. Gorgeously shot, with terrific production values and fine acting (especially by Jonathan Scarfe, who makes a compelling and charismatic Joseph Smith), these films have terrific messages about faith, testimony, forgiveness, sacrifice, and familial loyalty. Though there are some flaws (occasionally sappy dialogue, a change of several key actors after the first film), the sheer artistry of the filmmaking and the power of the storytelling make these worth the watch.

GRADE: B+

CONTENT OVERVIEW: A man is whipped for his beliefs (off screen, but we hear the whipping and the shouting and afterward see the scars). Some punches are thrown. Villainous types drink whiskey. Joseph Smith is tarred and feathered.

MESSAGES TO DISCUSS: God the Father and his Son Jesus Christ appeared to Joseph Smith to usher in the Restoration of the gospel (Joseph Smith—History 1:3–20). "Happiness in family life is most likely to be achieved when founded upon the teaching of the Lord Jesus Christ. Successful marriages and families are established and maintained on principles of faith, prayer, repentance, forgiveness, respect, love, compassion, work, and wholesome recreational activities" ("The Family: a Proclamation to the World," *Ensign*, Nov. 1995, 102).

WRECK-IT RALPH (PG, 2012)

A grin-inducing mix of humor, heart, and retro nostalgia, Disney's *Wreck-It Ralph* does for video games what *Toy Story* did for playthings: it humanizes them by taking a peek inside their "secret world." The film follows the quest of a lonely 8-bit villain who jumps from game to game to try and prove that he can be a hero. Although it starts with an overly simple story and leans, amusingly if a tad too-heavily, on video game in-jokes, the film evolves into a clever tale of friendship and selflessness. Its various story threads come together smartly, it's very funny, and its character arcs culminate in a touching fashion (I'm always embarrassed when "kids' movies" make me tear up). With creative character design and animation as well as excellent vocal work, *Wreck-It Ralph* is a can't-lose family night movie, even if you're not a gamer.

GRADE: A-

CONTENT OVERVIEW: It has no language or sexuality. There are a few childishly crude jokes and instances of name-calling ("booger-face," etc.), as well as mild video game–related violence.

MESSAGES TO DISCUSS: No matter who you are or what you've done, it's never too late to change and do what's right (Alma 26:17–22).

YOUNG VICTORIA, THE (PG, 2009)

The Young Victoria is a dramatically gripping depiction of the early years of Queen Victoria, from her youth when politicians and royalty tried to use her as a pawn, through her metamorphosis into a bold and virtuous ruler who would not be pushed around. Emily Blunt gives a marvelously layered performance in the title role, capturing all of the nuances of this complex and dynamic historical figure while making her into a fully-realized human being. Rupert Friend does fine work as her husband, Prince Albert; they have a wonderful "give and take" chemistry together that makes this one of the most enjoyable on-screen romances in years. Lush cinematography; an intelligent, witty, and emotionally engaging screenplay; and solid supporting performances make this a must-see period film.

GRADE: A

CONTENT OVERVIEW: A husband and wife kiss in bed on their wedding night (clothed). The scene ends there, and we see them the morning after, clothed and happy; sex is implied, but nothing is shown and the matter is handled in good taste. There is one mild profanity. A man takes a bullet for a woman; we see some blood on his arm but it's not excessive. A man screams at and intimidates a woman in front of her mother.

MESSAGES TO DISCUSS: Husbands are to love their wives and give of themselves for them (Ephesians 5:25). Benevolent rulers can bring to pass much good in the lives of their subjects (Mosiah 29:13–15).

Indexes

GENRE

ACTION/ADVENTURE

ANIMATED

DRAMA

FANTASY/SCI-FI

HALLOWEEN

MUSICAL (*SEE ALSO* ANIMATED)

RELIGIOUS (LDS)

RELIGIOUS (OTHER)

ROMANCE

GOSPEL TOPIC

DEBT

DEATH (COPING WITH)

ENEMIES, LOVE TOWARD

FAITH

FAMILIES

GIFTS, TALENTS

HUMOR

IMAGINATION

JESUS CHRIST

KNOWLEDGE

MARRIAGE

NATURE

OBEDIENCE

OVERINDULGENCE

PARENTS

PRAYER

PREJUDICE, TOLERANCE

PROMPTINGS (FOLLOWING)

PROPHETS, APOSTLES, REVELATION

TRIALS, TRIBULATIONS

UNITY

WARFARE, FIGHTING (RIGHTEOUS)

WEAKNESSES (MADE STRONG)

WORD OF WISDOM

RATING

NOT RATED

About the Author

Jonathan Decker is a licensed marriage and family therapist specializing in couples' therapy and singles' guidance. He has a background in stage and film performance, appearing in numerous independent movies (most notably the feature-length *24* parody *CTU: Provo*, co-starring Donny Osmond and *The Testaments'* Rick Macy) as well as writing and performing for the popular BYU comedy group Divine Comedy. Jonathan hosts a weekly segment on classic and overlooked films on *The KJZZ Movie Show* on KJZZ-TV in Utah. He also has a weekly entertainment column with *Meridian Magazine* (www.ldsmag.com) and writes reviews of current Hollywood films on his website, www.mormonmovieguy.com. Jonathan lives with his wife and children in St. George, Utah.